'LADY, YOU'RE NOT A MAN!'

Apurva Purohit is the CEO of Radio City 91.1 FM and an IIMB alumnus. She is one of the very few women CEOs in the media and entertainment space in India and has been managing media organizations for a large part of the twenty-five years she has spent in the corporate world.

While Apurva has nothing against men and is, indeed, quite fond of them, she believes that women are equally competent (and sometimes more so!) and they need to start grabbing a larger part of the sky for themselves.

You can connect with Apurva at:

- allwomenatwork@gmail.com
- www.twitter.com/apurva_purohit
- www.facebook.com/LadyYoureNotaMan
- www.womenatwork.co.in

'LADY, YOU'RE NOT A MAN!'

THE ADVENTURES OF A WOMAN AT WORK

APURVA PUROHIT

RUPA

Published by
Rupa Publications India Pvt. Ltd 2013
7/16, Ansari Road, Daryaganj
New Delhi 110002

Sales centres:
Allahabad Bengaluru Chennai
Hyderabad Jaipur Kathmandu
Kolkata Mumbai

ISBN: 978-81-291-2904-8

Fifth impression 2014

10 9 8 7 6 5

The moral right of the author has been asserted.

Typeset by Jojy Philip, New Delhi.

Printed at Thomson Press India Ltd, Faridabad

To
Mummy,
Sanjay and Siddharth

CONTENTS

PROLOGUE

Yeeks! I wake up with a start as the alarm goes off shrilly next to me. It's 5.30 a.m., and I need a full hour more to complete my recommended sleep quota. But here I am, pounding heart, buzzing nerves, eyes wide open because of that blasted alarm. The person for whom it is intended is blissfully unaware of the commotion, snoring mellifluously (he is an accomplished singer, and thus even snores in sur) next to me. I nudge him, with little effect and to no avail.

The alarm rings again at 5.45 a.m., and then again at 6 a.m. Finally, Husband Dearest (HD, for future reference) slowly wakes up from his beauty sleep and starts the long and detailed preparation for his morning walk.

I have been unsuccessfully agitating against this concept of setting a pre-alarm half an hour prior to the main alarm for several years. According to me, if you have to get up at 6 a.m., the alarm should be set at 5.55 a.m.; however, HD claims that the pre-alarm is extremely critical to awaken his subconscious from deep slumber—post which, I gather, he needs another forty-five minutes to get the rest of him up and going.

Me? I need just an instant to be fully awake, having left the luxury of taking hours to get up behind me a long time ago, somewhere around the time that my son was born.

Rapidly firing instructions at the maid, screaming 'Siddharth, wake up, your bus will be here in thirty minutes!' and brushing my teeth at the same time, I rush around trying to catch up with the day that already seems to be running an hour ahead of me.

The next half hour is a frenzy of packing lunch, looking for lost homework and missing shoelaces (I don't know what Sid does, but every day he loses one lace; I think he eats them in lieu of the lunch I pack). The dhobi has decided to come at this precise moment to settle his bill, the maid is having hysterics because the gas is over, the dog is barking and I can hear the bus honking at the building gate.

Sid and I rush out, waving frantically to the driver who has decided to punish us for our daily tardiness by not waiting for more than thirty seconds. We run behind the bus, shouting for him to stop, aided ably by the newspaper boy, the loitering street urchin and an obliging neighbour. Our combined vocal power works—the bus driver can no longer pretend that he hasn't heard us. The bus, protesting and unwilling, screeches to a halt. I thrust Sid in, along with his bag, water bottle and half-eaten toast, ignore the muttered imprecations of the driver and, heaving a sigh of relief, trudge back home.

Barely have I flopped down at the table and pulled the paper towards me when in walks HD, rosy-cheeked and bushy-tailed, rubbing his hands together. 'So, having a relaxed, cosy read? What's for breakfast?'

While I am debating between biting his head off and throwing the paper at him, the phone rings. It's one of our investors and board members. 'Have you seen the business paper today? Competition has announced their quarterly results and they have grown 0.325 times more than your organization. What's your take on this?'

I want to say: 'Buddy, it's 8.30 in the morning, I haven't had so much as a sip of coffee, I feel as if I have already run a marathon and looming ahead is a day replete with expectant husband, hysterical maid, a regional head who quit last night and two meetings with government officials who don't want to take any decision on anything—and you want my take?' But better sense prevails. Promising to get back to him in a couple of hours, I rise from the dining table and steel myself to face yet another day in the life of that beleaguered species, the working woman.

Staggering through several such days and nights in a career spanning twenty-odd years of being wife, mom and boss, somewhere down the line, I figured out that you have to first start off by doing a reality check and accepting certain basic truths about yourself. You need to begin by acknowledging the problems that come with being a working mom, the guilt that is a constant companion in whatever you do, the balance you try to find between a cantankerous and ill child and an important presentation, and the fact that, however much you try, you just can't be superwoman. And then life becomes easier.

You learn to adapt, to use whatever help and resources you can access, to adjust and, more importantly, teach your family to adjust. Finally, in the long haul, come achievement and a sense of accomplishment—hard won, but oh so sweet!

I want to share this journey with you, so that you don't feel that you are out there all alone, juggling work and home, navigating the treacherous corridors of the corporate world all by yourself.

And, who knows, as we set off on this adventure, we may both learn something new…

Part I

ACCEPTANCE

Before any great achievement comes the acceptance of your particular reality—and then you learn to adapt to it, to use it to excel and fly.

1

LADY, YOU'RE NOT A MAN!

CHANDNI AND CHAMELI

'Chandni, your parents must have named you with such tender expectations, fondly imagining that you would be gentle, feminine, graceful. The name conjures up such evocative images of soft moonlit nights, chiffon drapes, a cool breeze wafting around...then why do you behave so much like a Sooraj? All hot and aggressive and dominating?' I asked my friend and senior colleague one day, gently nudging her towards the ladies' loo and away from the men's toilet which she was absentmindedly about to enter.

'What bloody nonsense you talk!' she growled, adjusting her hypothetical balls as she marched into the office. 'Oye, you fucker! Have you finished the presentation I asked for?' She glared at the executive waiting for her and shivering with fright. The poor fellow had actually done the work, but he was so scared of her that he could only stutter a yes before handing her the printouts and scurrying off.

If you saw Chandni, it became quite apparent that she had rejected the notion that she had been born without the Y chromosome. Short hair, boxy jacket with trousers, swaggering around with her hands perpetually in her pockets, smoking furiously, was the vision that was Chandni. The only thing missing was a scarf a la Amitabh Bachchan around her neck. She certainly got her work done with this approach, and people around were terrified of her, but I also found her constantly on edge, trying to be something she was not.

The fact is that women of her generation had to break the glass ceiling by being manlier than the men around. After all, the only role models that existed then were male, and thus to get ahead you emulated them by being ball-breakers. Bra-burning was not only a sign of liberation but also a signal that women were ready to play in the boys' part of the playground, according to their rules of the game.

(This is not to say that women cannot be aggressive or vocal. Many women are, and that's fine—I'm talking about assuming a persona that does not come naturally to you.)

While corporate India, especially during the first wave of female emancipation, was sprinkled with several Chandnis, it unfortunately also had (and continues to have) women who, like the Chameli vine, believed that they had to cling to the big strong male to survive.

Whereas the Chandnis of the world, as the front guard in breaking the walls that were hemming women in, had a reason for being strident and aggressive, I personally feel that the Chameli type of women have no excuse to behave as they do. They love to play damsels in distress, always looking for a knight in shining armour to ride to their rescue. They believe that smouldering looks and a deep cleavage are the strongest assets they have, and try to use feminine wiles to get what they want. Unfortunately, by doing so, they demean themselves and their competence.

I remember my early days in advertising, when there

were these senior women media marketers who used to sell advertising space for magazines. They were very clear about the 'P' in their marketing—'patao' the client and get the business. I have actually seen someone unbutton the top two buttons of her shirt before going in for a meeting, I kid you not. And, of course, the sari pallu which artlessly slips off is something we have all encountered.

Otherwise fairly capable at their work, during a crisis situation, a few women suddenly decide to become weak-kneed heroines who require help from their bosses to complete an overdue presentation or deal with a particularly tough client. Alternatively, they begin to play at being the office spouse, cosying up to male superiors. 'Have you eaten?' 'Can I get you a cup of tea?' All this as they bat their eyelashes coyly. Many men love all this attention since it panders to their sense of self-worth; most will go charging on their white steeds to solve the problem, not realizing that they are being taken advantage of.

But every time a woman does this, I wonder if she realizes that she is only reinforcing the stereotype of women being wilting flowers and incapable of dealing with the big, bad corporate world all by themselves and, in the process, doing herself and her sisters immeasurable harm.

I don't think either morphing into a man or becoming a damsel in constant distress is the route to success today. Fortunately, with more women around, things have changed and slowly a new breed of women managers is emerging, people who are as comfortable with being feminine (without overdoing it) as they are with being efficient taskmasters. They celebrate the softer touch they are able to bring to managing people, the consensus-building approach they have in decision-making and the emotional connect they can forge with their colleagues. And they do so without being ashamed of their hormones, emotions or nurturing nature. (PMS is part and parcel of our lives—so what if we get mood swings once in a while?)

Many women come to me and say that they have often embarrassed themselves because inadvertently they have cried at some point or other at work. Now, you know that women cry for all sorts of reasons. They cry when they are angry or when their cup overflows with joy. They cry when they read a soppy letter from an old boyfriend or get an out-of-turn promotion. When they are bitter about a break-up, when they watch a Karan Johar film, when someone finally applauds them, when someone treats them unfairly. Statistics say that a typical woman will cry for fourteen months in her lifetime. I, for example, invariably cry while watching sad movies (and get laughed at by my family).

Letting your emotions show is not a big deal, and there's no harm done in the long term if once in a rare while the waterworks overflow at office. But the key thing to remember here is the word 'rare'. Just because it is okay to show emotion does not mean you can become a watering pot—you do, at the end of the day, want to be treated with seriousness and respect.

Deepika, a colleague of mine, used to be an overly sensitive soul and a major crier in her youth. She once cried all the way home after a bad day at work and the poor cab driver was so overwhelmed that he refused to take the fare from her. However, today she has turned her sensitivity into a strength and is one of the most empathetic and successful managers I know.

So, dear ladies, the first lesson of acceptance is to admit to ourselves that there is nothing wrong with being a woman, and the entire package that comes along with it—volatile feelings, soft heart, sharp tongue, belly fat, et al! However, let's also not use parts of the package to take undue advantage of men. It's not playing fair, and it affects attitudes not just towards individuals but also the whole sex.

With that as the starting point, let's go out and wow everyone with our talent, our empathy and our feminine style. And while we do that maybe we also need to thank the Chandnis who came before us and burnt their bras so that we could wear our lacy ones triumphantly.

CORPORATE MANTRA OF THE DAY

- Be confident in your femininity. Don't apologize for being a woman, and accept yourself as you are. Mood swings and crying jags once in a while are fine. (But don't do it too often, please!)

PSST...

- If you *have* to bat your eyelashes and show a bit of leg to get what you want, can you please be more subtle? The guys may not figure it out, but I assure you that the women around you do catch on!

2

LEARNING TO LIVE WITH GUILT

WHICH GUILT ARE YOU COMFORTABLE WITH?

A young lady walked up to me the other day, all teary-eyed and unhappy. 'I am planning to quit my job. I can't bear to see my three-year-old daughter cry every morning when I leave for work,' she whispered to me.

I questioned her and gathered that she was an extremely successful young woman with a management degree from one of the IIMs and currently working with a big consultancy firm. As is the norm in these places, she took home a very fat pay cheque and was climbing up the ladder quite speedily. But it appeared that she was willing to trade in all of that for her daughter.

Having gone through many such moments in my own life, I completely empathized with the conflicting emotions she was facing. In fact, it is a quandary that every working woman has confronted many times in her career—it is especially problematic for working moms with young children.

Every time Sid would fall ill and I had to leave him at home, or there was some crisis at work which required several days and nights of not being home for dinner, I would go into paroxysms of guilt and want to quit my job immediately. This invariably caused tremendous consternation at home, with both HD and Sid horrified at the prospect of having me at home 24x7 and hovering around them all the time.

Sid, being a wise child, never directly opposed me. Instead, he would gently bring up the advantages of having a working mom by telling me solemnly, 'See how independent I have become, so much better than my friends at managing by myself.' If that didn't cut any ice, 'I really appreciate the space you have given me and allowed me to grow, Mom.' (Laying it on a bit thick, if you ask me, but so sweetly put.) HD, however, would revolt bluntly against the very thought of me being at home. 'You will either keep calling me at work, wanting to talk and bond with me, or, worse, with no outlet for all that bossiness, you will want to take over and manage the lives of all our extended family, friends and neighbours and drive all of them nuts.' (I like to call it my natural leadership style, but you know how husbands are.) And then he would totter to the bar to pour himself a large drink to recover from the imminent nightmare. (You would have thought I was suggesting becoming a serial killer or something.)

Taking all of this into consideration, and thinking about everything calmly, luckily I always decided against those momentary impulses.

I counselled the guilt-ridden young lady by telling her that in leaving her job all she would be doing would be exchanging one type of guilt for another.

I have many friends who gave up work to take care of their children. While there is nothing wrong with doing so, I haven't seen any lessening of guilt in their case. The only difference is that instead of feeling guilty for leaving their child behind, they are now feeling guilty for wasting their education and the degrees they worked so hard at getting.

The question to ask, then, is: which guilt are you more comfortable with? Because being guilt-free is a no-option for a woman. If you are not feeling guilty about leaving your kid when you go off to work, you are feeling guilty about missing that office party where you could have dazzled the boss with your wit and repartee, since you had to rush home to finish your child's school project. If you are feeling thrilled because of a brilliant strategy presentation you just made, you are simultaneously feeling guilty about the endless Maggi meals you served your family in the week preceding the presentation. And so it goes on.

One day, in one of my gloomier moods, convinced that I was a terrible mother, I asked Sid whether he had felt abandoned when I had left him with my mother for an entire week when he had chicken pox. We had an urgent pitch going on and I was working all hours of the day—there was no way I would have been able to manage him, the chicken pox and the pitch. Sid was surprised by my question. 'Of course not, Mom! What's the matter with you? All I remember is having a great time with a week off from school, and Nani telling me stories while I lay in bed. Only, all that itching was a bit painful.'

This discussion took place some ten years post the event— all the while, I had been flailing myself, the chicken pox episode being an important component of my self-portrait titled 'A Horrible Mom'. And that's when I realized that it is we mothers who keep holding on to our perceived flaws, carrying them around as a basketful of regrets. Our children have (mostly) long forgotten, forgiven and moved on.

I remember reading this sweet story about a mother who constantly felt guilty about not getting her son ready in time for school because she would end up organizing everything at the last minute, including giving him a hastily ironed shirt moments before he left for school...till she read what he had written in a school essay on happiness: 'Happiness is wearing a warm, freshly ironed shirt on a cold winter morning!'

Lesson number two in the path to acceptance, therefore, is to not fight against the guilt monster but accept it as part and parcel of your life, a beast that will constantly follow you wherever you go and whatever you do.

If you are going to feel guilty anyway, you may as well do so for something which also makes you feel good about yourself. Like continuing being a working mom!

CORPORATE MANTRA OF THE DAY

- You certainly have a right to choose to be either a working mom or a stay-at-home mom, depending on your particular circumstances and situation. Unfortunately, feeling or not feeling guilty is not a choice you can make, since guilt comes along as part of the territory of being a woman.
- The only choice you can make is to decide which guilt you want to live with. The guilt of compromising on always being around for your kids and family, or the guilt of wasting that potential and that education?

PSST...

- Sometimes, there are compensations for all that guilt—in the same way that the guilt of not following the diet plan is accompanied by the joy of eating pani-puri! Enjoy the good things that come with the guilt of being a working mom. Financial independence, for instance. Or the fact that you can indulge yourself and your children once in a while with the money that you have earned.

3

LIFE IS INDEED UNFAIR

THEY SAY IT'S A MAN'S WORLD

Suchitra and Bobby Dalal comprise a typical upper-middle-class couple in most respects except one. Like many of their contemporaries, they met at work, dated for a bit and then got married. Vihaan was born three years down the line, and they recently celebrated their twelfth wedding anniversary, having been happily married for those years. He is an architect and she is the HR head at a leading bank. A double income ensures the added benefit of a lovely flat in the centre of town, foreign holidays and international schooling for Vihaan. So all is well and as it should be in the Dalal household.

The one thing that makes them different from everyone else around them is that when Vihaan was born, since Bobby was in a position to manage his career by being a part-time consultant, and Suchitra was the higher earner of the two, they took the brave decision of Bobby becoming the primary parent and caregiver of the baby.

I am not talking about parenting at the superficial level, like Bobby dropping and picking up Vihaan from school and scolding him once in a while for not studying (which many fathers believe immediately qualifies them to boast that they are in charge of their children's upbringing). The Dalals went the whole hog, with Bobby giving up his job and doing consultancy assignments from home. He took over complete charge of Vihaan, from getting him ready for school to packing his lunch to taking him for football practice. He manages home and hearth and birthday parties and dentist appointments—and Suchitra concentrates completely on her job, with such able support at home!

Now, you would think that all their friends and acquaintances (especially female) would laud this decision and hold up Bobby as a beacon of emancipation, pointing him out to husbands, brothers and sons as someone they should emulate. But, shockingly, that's not the case at all. Sample a conversation I overheard between two of their catty neighbours who were at a birthday party that Bobby and Vihaan were attending.

Kitty A (busily checking her mobile): 'Who is this Anna woman? Anna Hazare? Do you know her? I keep on getting messages to join her march or something. Is she some Delhi-type socialite you think?'

Kitty B: 'Never heard of her. But forget that. Look, there's Bobby again with Vihaan. This is the third time I'm seeing him bringing their son to an afternoon party. Where is Suchitra? Has she left him or something?'

'I believe she travels a lot, given that high-flying job of hers, you know,' snickered Kitty A.

Kitty B sniffed. 'That's all very well, but what about him? Doesn't he have a job to go to? Or this recession-vecession has ensured he doesn't have one? Do you think I should ask DK to help him?'

(Have you noticed how wives of many 'powerful' men call their husbands by their initials? I think it is something to do with all those weapons being called by acronyms, like AK-47, MIG-20, etc. There is clearly some subliminal referencing going on here.)

'Well, I don't know about that, but one thing is very clear. She is the one who wears the pants in the house. See that hangdog expression on his face? Let's go and cheer him up, poor fellow.' And off waltzed Kitty A towards Bobby.

It was obviously inconceivable to these women that Bobby had taken a deliberate decision to be a stay-at-home father; clearly, it must have been out of having no choice in the matter! And, immediately, in their eyes, he had become the lesser partner in the marriage.

Imagine, then, how women possibly demean their own selves by projecting a stay-at-home parent's role as a lesser one; and imagine the enormous bias a man needs to overcome if he decides that he doesn't want to be the primary wage earner and provider for the family and encourages his wife to be so.

Many women get into a discussion with me on how everything in the corporate workplace is structured around males: like the boys' club which goes drinking after work every day, whereas women have to rush straight home to their second job; or the smoking alcove and the men's loo, where male colleagues can network and bond with the boss. They complain how life is so unfair, particularly for women who want both a home and a career—they have to do twice the work and make twice the effort to ensure that they are not compromising one for the other, while men just focus on their jobs since most of them have someone at home to pack their lunch dabbas and take care of the PTA meetings.

No doubt they are right about several aspects, but I ask these women to also pause for a moment and consider whether life is as hunky-dory as they think it is for men.

Just as women have been labelled into doing things that

restrict them, men too have been tightly boxed in by society into the role they have to play: that of the primary provider and protector of the family. So, whether he likes it or not, a typical middle-class man has to get up every morning and ensure he takes care of his family and their needs. A long commute, a bad boss, a dead-end job—nothing is acceptable as an excuse for him to one day just throw up his hands and declare, 'I'll stay at home and take care of the kids, you work!' While many women can and do just that.

A woman can get up one day and say, 'I want to leave my job and stay at home and explore my creative side. I will learn painting and pottery and also be a good mother to my child.' She may be running away from a nasty boss or a high-pressure project, but no one will point a finger at her. Instead, she will be seen as a martyr and a great mother who 'sacrificed' her career for the sake of her family. Ask yourselves this: can a man do the same? And, if he does, will he get the same respect he got as the chief provider and earner?

A friend's father retired recently, and he inadvertently realized that his importance in the household had diminished almost overnight. For the last thirty-odd years, his wife had been asking him what he would like made for dinner every night; but from the day he retired, she stopped asking him and instead started asking her son (who had now become the primary earner in the house). It was heart-wrenching to see the stunned look on the father's face when he realized the subtle shift in power that had taken place.

Before we complain about how life is so unfair to us and how men are so much better off, let us ask ourselves whether this is really true. Men are as much victims of the roles that have been written for them by society as we are. And woe betide the man who wants to change the script and explore his nurturing nature as opposed to his earning role!

Life is indeed unfair, but it is pretty democratic in its unfairness. In some way or another, life will be unfair to everyone, whatever their colour, caste, creed or gender. So, let's accept this fundamental reality and move on.

And while we figure out how to improve the fairness quotient for ourselves, let's take a moment to feel sympathy for the men around us, who too have their own crosses to bear.

CORPORATE MANTRA OF THE DAY

- Many of us waste a lot of time bemoaning the unfairness of life, as if it has dealt a particularly bad hand only to us. The fact is that everyone has a few dud cards somewhere in their deck.
- While it may seem that life has been unjust largely to women and men have everything going their way, the reality is not so. Men too have numerous challenges they face—the key one being that they can't easily escape the societally designated role of being the family's chief wage earner.

PSST...

- I know your husband may not be the knight in shining armour you dreamt of, but once in a while appreciate him for the dragons he slays every day for you—even if they take the form of cockroaches in the bathroom.
- If you know a Bobby in your life, do make sure that you go up and compliment him for being a part of that rare breed of 'complete men'.

4

BOYS WILL BE BOYS
(AND GIRLS WILL DO ALL
THE HARD WORK)
THE MULTITASKING GENE

While on the subject of men, and in the true spirit of feminine benevolence having realized that they too have to deal with many biases, I think I owe it to the sisterhood to also acknowledge that there are certain undesirable facets of these poor dear creatures that we may have no choice but to accept. And one of them is that they just can't multitask—and thus we end up doing all the extra work!

Down the line, when you are running around managing your new promotion, your child's homework, obnoxious relatives (from his side of the family, not yours) dropping in unexpectedly, burst pressure cooker rings and subordinates who want to be motivated just to come to office on time, somewhere in that rigmarole you will realize that invariably you are the one picking up all the additional burden. And your spouse is either busy reading the newspaper and giving his opinion on the government's inefficiencies or focusing fully on the latest crisis at work or wholeheartedly centring his thoughts to be in tune with Sachin Tendulkar's as he goes out to bat for his next century! While you run around in multiple circles, he is very clearly jogging on a single linear track, chasing one—and only one—thing at a time.

I tell my family: 'Okay, guys, I'm going out for a couple of hours. By the time I come back, please finish Sid's packing and take the dog out for a walk. The newspaper boy will come, pay his bill and heat up the food.' Knowing their propensity to dilly-dally, I have cleverly given them tasks which have a non-negotiable expiration time; after all, Sid has to catch the six o'clock flight, the dog will pee in the house if not taken outside and everyone has to eat lunch! Satisfied at my masterful and cunningly planned delegation, I waltz off.

I come back after one hour and fifty-five minutes (typical of any normal efficient woman, when I commit a particular time I mean it) and open the door to utter chaos. The dog is whimpering frantically with a bladder that is ready to burst, Sid's clothes are lying haphazardly on the floor, the food is congealing on the table and every television set in the house is blaring away. While Sid (wearing just a shirt and nothing else), HD (unfathomably wearing two knotted ties around his neck) and the newspaper boy are sitting in front of one of the televisions with their mouths agape.

'Hullo? What the hell is going on?' I shout to make myself heard over the din of three TVs and Harsha Bhogle's hysterical voice. There is no visible sign that anyone has heard me, apart from the dog, who starts jumping and nudging me agitatedly towards the door. I try again: 'Hullooo?'

'Ssh!' All three glare at me. 'India's batting.'

'Huh?' I am quite perplexed. Is there a World Cup final

going on that I am not aware of? Or an India-Pakistan one-day match? 'Excuse me, guys. Can you kindly explain what is going on? Why you haven't done a single chore I asked you to do?' I walk to the TV set and switch it off decisively.

'Aww, shucks, Mom, why did you come back so soon?' grumbles Sid.

HD glares at me. 'It was a very important match we were watching you know. India-Australia in 1998, one of the best knocks by Sachin!'

The newspaper boy joins the communal censuring by sniffing disparagingly at me.

I goggle. 'Are you telling me that for the last two hours you have been sitting doing nothing but watch a re-run of a match you have probably seen seventy-five times? And when there is so much to do? Sid has a flight to catch in the next three hours—did that fact get lost somewhere in the innumerable cricket statistics that occupy your minds so deeply?' I query sarcastically.

'Of course not, we have also been doing Sid's packing, can't you see?' HD frowns, flinging his arms around.

'No, I can't see!' I explode. 'There are exactly two folded shirts in the suitcase. Why are the rest of the clothes lying around? And why are you wearing two ties?'

'I was teaching Sid how to knot them and he's been trying on all his clothes first to see which fit him and which don't so that we don't waste space in the suitcase.'

My son and my husband both look at me, challenging me to question their faultless logic. My head starts reeling. Why on earth would anyone want to try out clothes which they have bought just a week ago to check for size? I sniff suspiciously—have they been drinking to celebrate this great knock of Sachin's, forgetting in the general euphoria that it took place fifteen years ago? But I can't find much evidence of any celebrations except for the fact that the newspaper boy is waving an India flag enthusiastically.

With a sigh of forbearance, I decide not to waste any more time in argument and start organizing lunch quickly so that I can finish the packing before the airport pick-up arrives. In the meantime, the dog has peed on the antique Afghan carpet; I turn around to ask them to clean the mess, only to realize that both of them have drifted away to the second TV and have zoned out yet again.

My family may not agree, but frankly I have no problem if they watch cricket, hockey, football, kabaddi, beach volleyball or whatever else they want, as long as they do it while doing their other chores. Most women I know—my sister, for one—can watch a TV serial, cook, keep an eye on my nephew and talk to my mom intelligently, all at the same time. So why can't any of the men I know do more than one thing at a time?

And that really is the crux of the matter. Women are born with the multitasking gene embedded in them, whereas men don't understand that concept at all. So, for example, when men are driving, that's all they can do. If they get a phone call, do you notice how the speed of their driving changes with the tone of the conversation? If they are arguing with someone, they will drive fast; if they are murmuring sweet nothings, the car too moves languidly. That's because they have a one-track mind, and everything has to fall in one singular rhythm for men to be able to make sense of it. Whereas a woman can simultaneously talk on the phone, peel an apple, write a memo and have a mental argument with her boyfriend.

No wonder, then, that women are so much more efficient and manage to get several more things done, whether at work or at home, than their male counterparts—and, undoubtedly, make better managers! They can deal with home, work, multiple projects and several crises adeptly and efficiently, all at the same time.

And because women can do more in less time, the fallout is that the distribution of labour is invariably skewed towards women. Men end up doing much less work because they just take so long to finish their tasks, one job at a time.

Should we then just accept that, by virtue of being more efficient, we will have to pick up the greater burden, or should we flail against this inequity too?

Personally, I have found it more practical to just manage most of the stuff myself; it takes less time than ensuring the guys do it right. The poor souls will anyway get more confused if you give them more than one simple instruction and end by messing everything up!

CORPORATE MANTRA OF THE DAY

- Multitasking is a unique skill, which mostly women have, and we should use it to the fullest capacity to move ahead in the race.
- Therefore, never walk away from accepting an additional project at work, and definitely take up the home-improvement tasks you have been planning alongside—it will only hone this skill better!

PSST...

- Doing twenty-three things at the same time is child's play for you, but make a big deal out of it and make sure you get your share of the compliments for being so organized and efficient.
- The trick in making men do work is to seamlessly fit it into their monotonic rhythm. So, 'Please buy the

milk while coming back from your walk' works. But, remember, only one instruction at a time. If you say 'Buy milk and fill gas', one of these chores will certainly not get done.

5

YOUR PROBLEMS ARE NOT UNIQUE
EVERYONE'S MOTHER-IN-LAW IS EVIL AND HUSBAND IS LAZY
THE SUFFERING SITA SYNDROME

Indians, as we all know, are big fans of Bollywood. In fact, Bollywood pervades our lives so totally that it is often considered a standalone religion with a fan base that is certainly larger than many other religions put together, and may one day overtake even Facebook.

Bollywood cuts across barriers of class, caste and creed, and has become a unifying cultural force which binds all of us together to worship at its altar (with Amitabh Bachchan's baritone chanting a hymn in its praise as the background score). I often imagine that, when Martians land on earth a few centuries down the line, there will be a curator showing them Meena Kumari's sindoor box, Gabbar's whip, Madhuri

Dixit's choli and Salman's torn shirt as totems to explain India's evolution.

Bollywood has become so ingrained in all of us that we don't recognize fact from fiction any longer and are completely muddled as to where our actual traditions and rituals begin, and where the ceremonies popularized by Bollywood end. This reality was brought home to me when I attended the wedding of a friend's daughter in Chennai recently.

My friend is from such a deeply conservative Tam-Brahm family that when I was studying with her in Chennai many years ago her father had expressly forbidden her from mixing with me: 'That North Indian girl will corrupt you. Haven't you seen she wears sleeveless blouses?' My poor friend's one act of rebellion had been to do exactly the opposite and continue her association with me. So, you can imagine my shock when the night before the usual 4 a.m. muhurutham at the kalyana mandapam, which I had expected, I was invited to a sangeet ceremony, which I had most certainly not expected. To my further amazement, the whole thing was a choreographed event with a song-and-dance routine and performances by the entire family. Including my friend's father (yes, the very same disapprover of sleeveless blouses) dancing to Dilip Kumar songs! And forget sleeves—most of the women were wearing itsy-bitsy bikini blouses with their Kanjivaram silks. All thanks to Bollywood weddings.

The fact that Bollywood can unite the North with the South and the East with the West and all of us with the North East is commendable, but there is one aspect of Bollywood which is certainly not praiseworthy and has negatively influenced an entire generation of women.

The unhappy truth is that when we were growing up the female leads in all Bollywood films were always portrayed as tragic and suffering souls. So, if they were not suffering because of being separated from unsuitable lovers by despotic fathers, they were suffering from being ill-treated by their thankless children. They suffered as poverty-stricken wives of farmers, as rich but neglected daughters of businessmen, as golden-hearted molls of smugglers, as discarded wives and as self-sacrificing call girls. Actresses in that era played a variety of roles, but invariably the leitmotif was suffering!

We saw all this repeatedly in cinemascopic effect and, more importantly, during our deeply susceptible teenage years; consequentially, Indian women of a certain age believe passionately that their fate is to suffer.

They suffer because they have mothers-in-law who trouble them, husbands who don't help them and children who are spoilt. They also suffer because they have bosses who don't recognize their talent and peers who bitch about them. They suffer in the 8.20 ladies' special and they suffer in the air-conditioned car. They suffer at home and then they come to work and suffer all over again!

Initially, I used to feel very sorry for these women, but slowly it dawned on me that many of them not only enjoy suffering but have made it into a vocation. And they often use it as a tool to emotionally blackmail people around them. So, even when absolutely nobody in the family is asking, they insist on making hot rotis at 10 p.m., after working the entire day. They do the laundry themselves instead of outsourcing it and stay back late at office to demonstrate how hard they are working instead of working a wee bit faster. They purposefully overburden themselves when it is actually both practical and feasible to delegate, or to not go to the extreme of grinding masalas themselves. All so that the next morning they can wear the thorny crown of martyrdom! They love being Suffering Sitas, because in their mind that is what an ideal Indian woman is supposed to be.

My cousin Gayatri is one of these perpetual sufferers and can easily beat everyone hollow in the tragedy queen up-man-ship game. I met her at a wedding recently.

'Hi, Gayatri, you are looking good—what a lovely sari!' I greeted her chirpily.

'Really?' Looking disparagingly down at herself, she said, 'It's one of the saris my mother-in-law gave me, second-hand you know. She didn't give me a single thing that was new when we got married. But I have never made a fuss or complained. What cannot be cured must be endured, I always say to myself.' She gazed at me mournfully with her slightly bulbous eyes.

Now, considering the entire family had heard Gayatri's lament over these second-hand things for the last decade, I didn't know how to respond. So I changed the topic. 'I just met Bittoo, he's growing into a fine young man. So tall...'

'Naturally.' She sniffed. 'I get up at 4.30 every morning and make a fresh mixture of dry fruits and aloe vera juice for him myself, in spite of my insomnia. You know how much I have suffered. I can't remember having a decent night's sleep in the last seven years. But a mother has to sacrifice something for her child, don't you think? And what is sleep, after all?'

I could see she was drifting away into movie-land, fondly imagining herself dressed in white, usurping Nirupa Roy's histrionic sacrificing-mother avatar. The atmosphere of maternal martyrdom had started becoming a little oppressive, so I decided to divert her attention into more positive avenues. 'Oh, look, the baraat is ready. Let's go and dance.'

'You go, you know I can't dance.' She looked at me reproachfully. 'After that epidural I took when Bittoo was born, my back has never been the same. Only I know the pain I suffer every moment of every day. But you go, you enjoy.

I'll just sit and watch.' She sighed as she sank gracefully into the nearest chair.

Feeling like a heel, I hastily disclaimed any desire to dance.

'I believe you have become CEO now? Imagine! And I was the one who always came first and beat you in class.' Gayatri tittered. 'Lucky you. But then you have such a good husband, he knows how to cook, doesn't he? And takes care of Sid when you travel? Really lucky, I must say. You know how useless Ramesh is. If I go out even for half an hour, he starts calling me on my mobile. And if I don't give him his morning tea with my own hands or make breakfast for him myself, he says his day doesn't go well at all. I can't even think of going back to work...otherwise, my boss used to say, "Gayatri, you will become MD for sure one day."' She looked tragic and valiant at the same time.

Feeling vaguely ashamed and guilty about having a supportive husband, no backache and no insomnia, I meekly ventured: 'How are your parents? Don't see them around.'

'Oh, they haven't come. Mummy had an upset stomach. She's suffered from poor digestion for years, you know...' (Suffering was obviously genetic in the family.) 'I made fresh food for them and delivered it to their house before coming here. Ramesh was so angry since we got late.'

'But, doesn't Aunty have a full-time cook?' I asked. As far as I knew, her mother had been lording it over a large and full-time retinue for several decades.

'They do, but I just didn't feel comfortable giving Mummy food cooked by someone else when she is unwell,' declared Gayatri piously.

The halo was glowing so brightly by now that it was threatening to blind me, so I pretended I had seen someone I knew and scuttled as far away as I could from all that nobility. There is just so much of forbearance one can take.

While suffering was no doubt considered noble once upon a time, I assure you that it is definitely passé now. (Besides, everything prior to the 1970s has become obsolescent or 'retro'.) Dishwashers, laundry services, readymade papads, pickles and masalas, cooks, chauffeurs and housecleaning services have obviously been designed to ease our burdens— and if we continue to forsake them in favour of carrying on our march to martyrdom, nobody will admire us. Instead, people will laugh at our foolishness in suffering when there is little reason to.

The Suffering Sita as an aspiration is just not fashionable any longer. The role will win us accolades no more, so let us graciously give up its ghost and let it rest in peace.

And, as we move into a more equal and confident era, let us look around for some better roles to play—roles which are positive and more fun for us. Like the sexy forty-something, the tough but classy boss, the spirited and enthusiastic executive or the coolly intelligent colleague!

CORPORATE MANTRA OF THE DAY

- In today's day and age, unnecessary suffering is no longer seen as noble; indeed, it is deemed downright impractical and foolish.
- There are several better and more fun parts we can choose to play now: the trendy mom, the sultry aunty, the chic diva, the suave HOD and the gracious boss, and so on. Check out the options, pick one that suits you and quit the suffering!

Psst...

- Indian men continue to have a very strong mother complex, so you may still be able to wring out a few more tears and benefits from the Suffering Sita model.

6

I DON'T NEED TO UNDERSTAND MORE THAN TWO BUTTONS
'ON' AND 'OFF'

IS THERE A CONCEPT SUCH AS STEREOTYPES?

I confess that I don't understand anything that is remotely (pun!) mechanical in nature. Any object that resembles a gadget scares the devil out of me, and I become a blithering idiot when faced with more than two buttons. So, when we were installing Tata Sky at home, I started hyperventilating on realizing that, horror of horrors, there would now be two remotes to deal with, each one having twenty-one buttons!

Eventually, I agreed to take a week's lessons from an impatient son and finally mastered switching on both the TV and the set top box simultaneously. I was just about feeling satisfied with my newly acquired skill when I got a frantic call one Saturday afternoon from HD. He wanted me to record a VIM—a Very Important Match. (I have yet to come across a match which has not been Very Important in my family's mind, much like all the guests at an awards function; every award show I have ever supervised invariably has only VIP guests who all need to be given the front row seats, along with special seating for their egos and assorted relatives.)

As HD started barking instructions at me, I immediately switched back to my idiot-personality, with my brain refusing to process anything he was saying. 'Apu, have you switched on the TV? Okay, are you on channel 402? Good, now press the record button... What? There is no record button? OF COURSE THERE IS A RECORD BUTTON! No, I am not shouting! Okay, okay, calm down. Can you see a little red button with R on it? Yes, that's the one. Now press it. Good girl. Has the recording symbol come on the screen? Where? WHAT DO YOU MEAN WHERE? On the TV screen, for God's sake! Acchha, please stop crying, will you? Look at the right-hand side top corner of the screen...'

Fortunately for my mental equilibrium and HD's vocal chords, Sid arrived just in time and all went well with the recording and the subsequent viewing.

Since I am in a confessional frame of mind today, let me also admit that I don't get the whole mystique surrounding cars. Or what distinguishes one from the other, or how to worship and respect them. Sometimes, even how to drive them. As far as I am concerned, a car is a mode of transport, very much like a bus or an auto, albeit more comfortable. So I just couldn't figure out why HD almost fainted when I pointed to a Tata Sumo the other day, mistaking it for his Audi. They were both big and black, after all. And when I was narrating this story to a couple of male friends, looking for sympathy for the pariah-like way HD had started treating me after the episode, they goggled and gasped as if I had committed the eighth cardinal sin and needed to be immediately consigned to the innermost circle of hell.

I also did not think there was any need whatsoever for them to roll on the floor in uncontrollable laughter. After all, it's not as if they are particularly bright with respect to cars themselves. Imagine drooling over the Aston Martin and the Mini Cooper—cars which can barely fit one person comfortably and with no leg or boot space. In fact, the aforementioned Audi has lesser leg room than the Accord we originally had, and I was quite shocked that it couldn't even accommodate eight people, given the price we paid for it. The cost has to translate into some visible benefit, like being able to fit in at least two families, their pets, their food hampers and assorted luggage, right? Otherwise why would you pay so much?

My ignorance with regard to cars became a matter of legend when the other day one of our male colleagues very proudly announced that he had bought a new car and we all decided to go out to celebrate the occasion. I got into the car and for the life of me couldn't figure out what compliments one pays a new car. Wow, what power? Ooh, great suspension? Outstanding reverberation? But since I am unfailingly polite, I had to say something. So I sniffed appreciatively and said, 'Aah, I love the smell of new leather.'

An ominous silence greeted my comment. It turned out that we were sitting in his three-year-old car, which was of a completely different make, colour, size and shape from the new purchase. After having excitedly extolled the virtues of the new car and having described it to me in the minutest detail, including telling me what the chassis number was, the poor man didn't know whether to laugh at me or strangle me.

So, because I don't understand cars and gadgets, am I an archetypical female with left-brain issues? I don't think so. I am, after all, very good with numbers and extremely logical and rational.

Are all men aggressive and power-hungry, with not a single empathetic bone in their bodies? Again, not true. HD, for instance, has always been the nurturer in our family. Apart from running a large organization, he also controls the kitchen in our house. He is a fabulous cook and has always ensured that the family gets a balanced meal every day. Left to me, we would have to make do with bread and eggs, with instant noodles once in a while to break the monotony.

And here's the clincher. I know quite a few men who are as challenged as I am with respect to automobiles. A male friend, for example, thought the Audi was a limited edition of some other car brand launched specifically for the Olympics because of the rings in the logo.

At a recent women leaders' conference, one of the panel members, who is a well-known educationist, made a point that women are typically not good at maths because they are right-brain dominant as compared to men. While she was using this to make a case that it is important for us to accept that there are differences between men and women, several women took umbrage. Her logic immediately had a score of women, many of them engineers and analysts, up in arms.

Certainly, in this day of the female finance whizz and the male metrosexual, the theory of males being left-brain dominant (and thus more logical and analytical) and women being more creative and less rational is collapsing both in business and social life. In our organization itself, two of the traditionally male posts—CFO and digital head—are held by women, while some of our male department heads spend hours counselling the women in their teams and hearing out all their problems, from marital issues to the best way to feed a newborn.

It is thus crystal-clear that traditional stereotypes are getting redefined and we cannot slot men and women into airtight boxes any longer. In fact, if you look closely, they are both actually learning from each other and picking up 'best practices', as we say in the management world, from one another.

It is worth mentioning here that I see more men picking up characteristics from women than the other way around! The evidence is all over for us to see. Today, there are far more male shoppers in malls, buying everything from clothes to shoes to spa treatments to skincare products. And if you enter one of those neighbourhood 'unisex' parlours, it is quite startling to see all shapes and sizes of men sprawled around, green goo on their faces, getting pedicures and chest-waxing and facials. A male friend I know has been known to go out to purchase a shirt and come back with a belt, a BlackBerry, a non-stick frying pan with a guarantee of twenty-five years and several tons of fruit—while his wife routinely finishes her annual apparel buying in fifteen minutes flat!

Clearly, this one-way transformation is yet another instance of the survival of the fittest. The fact is that the skills women have—of consensus-building, nurturing and listening—are the ones that are going to drive success in today's world, and not the leader-follower linear approach which men typically adopt.

Various theories and rumours suggest that one day men will just cease to exist: women have already become experts at every task necessary for human survival, and once they cross the final hurdle—single-handed reproduction—men won't be required any longer; at such a point in time, nature will take its due course and the male species will become extinct.

I certainly think this will happen, but in a slightly different fashion. Unlike dinosaurs, which suddenly vanished as a species one fine morning, men will slowly evolve into women.

Based on the evolutionary game that is unfolding before our eyes, my dear ladies, the lesson here is slightly spiritual in nature. It is this: cultivate patience, accept that our day will come, and wait for it. All empirical evidence shows that the world is moving in the direction we want—stereotypes disappearing, and men breaking free of the chrysalis of chauvinism and maybe even morphing into women one day.

So, throw away those cudgels, my sisters. It is only a matter of time. Stay calm, and remember: they also serve who only stand and wait.

CORPORATE MANTRA OF THE DAY

- Traditional stereotypes, both masculine and feminine, are slowly blurring and disappearing.
- In the dance of evolution, both sexes are borrowing characteristics from each other to help them survive in the changing world.

PSST...

- In the emerging world, the skills that are associated with women are going to be more important for survival than the traits that men are usually credited with. Men may have no choice but to morph into women!

7

CAN MEN BREAST-FEED?

THE BABY TRAP

We have now reached a little more than the mid-point in our journey of accepting the realities that come with being a working woman. We have learnt to accept the fact that we are women, not faded copies of men, with our own special strengths and weaknesses. We have understood that life is going to have its share of unfairness distributed amongst both sexes. We know now that as mothers we are going to constantly feel guilty, no matter what. We accept that men, like us, have several problems that they too grapple with on a daily basis (though, of course, they do have fundamental issues such as not being able to multitask and thus lead extremely inefficient lives). And since, along with Mr Darwin, we also know that only the fittest survive, we recognize that men will quietly evolve into women in the not-very-distant future. So, where do we go from here?

I would like to draw your attention now to a relatively tough circumstance that most working women around the age of thirty have to deal with.

Let me introduce you to Amrita, an extremely smart corporate lawyer who works on some of our legal cases. Amrita passed out of National Law School and, as a topper, got immediately placed with a leading law firm in Delhi; being hardworking, intelligent and sincere ensured that her career took off rapidly. By the time she was twenty-six, her parents had started making noises about getting her married. Since she too was not averse to the idea, a suitable boy was found and, with all the necessary pomp and splendour required of a Punjabi wedding, Amrita and Mohit happily started their journey of marital bliss. Five years passed by quite quickly, in a medley of hard work, parties, holidays, EMIs and a rapid climb up the corporate ladder for both of them.

Amrita is going to be thirty-two soon and is acutely aware that her biological clock is ticking away. One by one, their friends have started dropping off the party circuit with the excuse of 'baby at home', and she senses a kind of incompleteness in her life now. The nesting instinct is in full force, and squalling and screaming little tots from whom she used to earlier run a mile have become sweet, cuddly little toys. In fact, Amrita and Mohit have been talking about having a baby for a year. But the timing never seems right. For half the previous year, Mohit was on an international assignment, flying back to India once a month or so; this year, Amrita is in line for the junior partner position that has opened up in her law firm. She is worried that if she declares she is pregnant not only will she lose the position but, worse, it will also go to her bitterest rival, Bala the Slimeball.

Mohit doesn't see what the problem is. 'Darling, if you want to have a baby, let's have one. I am game. In fact, why not make a start tonight? There's a nice bottle of wine chilling away in the fridge. What do you say?' He wiggles his eyebrows teasingly at her.

'Uff, please be serious for once, Mohit. It's easy for you to say. But there's so much to think about and plan before we bring a baby into this world. It's a big responsibility you know,' Amrita chides.

'Come on, do you think I don't understand?' Mohit is hurt.

'No, it's not that. But how will we manage, who will take care...' Amrita trails off, woebegone.

Puzzled, Mohit says, 'But I thought both sets of parents have been making not-so-subtle offers that they are willing and able to babysit? So what's the issue?'

'But I'll have to go through the whole pregnancy bit, won't I? Can anyone else do that for me?' retorts Amrita sarcastically.

By now Mohit is utterly confused. She started this conversation—if she wants a baby, how else is it going to happen? And if she doesn't want one, why are they having this conversation?

And poor muddled-up Amrita cannot quite explain the resentment she is feeling. Because she does love him so, and it's not his fault and there is really nothing he can do.

Amrita wants a baby, but she also realizes that she is the one who will have to put a temporary hold on her career. It may last only as long as her maternity leave, or extend to months or years, but there will certainly be a break. And she resents that this onus will be on her and not on Mohit. After all, the baby will be his too, won't it? Then why does she have to take the break in her job? And possibly lose out on her promotion? (She can see the slimy Bala gloating already—when she gets back after her break, no matter what the length, he will be sitting in a cabin and she in a cubicle.)

The fact is that when it comes to baby-making—as the

primary manufacturer, so to speak—the responsibility of creation shifts to the woman completely. The husband is at best an OEM (Original Equipment Manufacturer) in the entire process, an individual-parts supplier. It is now that, for the first time, women who have been in an equal-partnership marriage find that they have to carry the heavier load. It can come as quite a shock, and can lead to all kinds of justifiable and not-so-justifiable resentment issues.

Just the other day, one of the executives in our office who had recently had a baby was telling me that the foremost thought in her mind on the delivery table was how to murder her husband—who, poor soul, was standing next to her, making placating sounds while she accused him of being the dastardly cause of all her suffering. (I believe 90% of all women hate their husbands the most when they are on the delivery table; it apparently comes second only to the wrath that follows the discovery that their husbands are having affairs with their twenty-six-year-old secretaries.)

The whole process of giving birth is quite a nasty one, however much your mother may have told you to the contrary, and actively disliking your husband during that period, I would say, is quite reasonable. Let me elucidate. (Note of caution: innocent vestal virgins and women who have not had babies yet, please skip the next two paragraphs; otherwise you may decide to remain in your current state of non-motherhood forever.)

There you are, lying on a cold table, like a beached whale, and desperately trying to remember your Lamaze exercises whilst various cheery-sounding doctors and nurses keep passing by, completely oblivious to your pain. If they do notice you, it is to come and check your levels of dilation; therefore, every once in a while someone pops by, inserts fingers up your nether regions and announces 'Only six inches, still a long while to go', absentmindedly pats you, and moves on. Many hours of agony and various random people looking up your legs later, a doctor finally strolls in and proclaims: 'Good, good, nine inches now. I think I'll be able to make it to the eight o' clock show. My wife has been very keen to watch this movie, I better not disappoint her. Otherwise canteen food for the whole of next week!' He laughs in what you consider a completely heartless fashion and starts washing up. You are convinced you are going to die and the doctor is discussing which movie he will watch. Callous bastard...just like that husband of yours...all men are rascals!

Unending hours of trauma later, when the baby is finally laid across your chest, there isn't right away that much-touted mystical feeling of bliss that transports you into maternal heaven. In fact, you look at the red-faced little tyke rather accusingly, given the indescribable pain you have gone through. Motherly love comes, of course, but later. You still have to go through the horror of several sleepless nights and the constant feeling of being a cow whose only job is to feed another human being who has no other purpose but to be fed and cleaned by you every two hours.

During the course of the baby saga, women end up resenting their husbands at periodic intervals, especially when they ask themselves some very fundamental questions. Like, why do I have to lose my figure when I have a baby? Why do I have to suffer morning sickness while he sits and stuffs everything he can see into his fat mouth? How come I have to stay at home in my current role as chief cow, whereas he continues his partying? The baby belongs to us both, doesn't it?

Sometimes this antipathy can build up to an unnecessary degree, causing a rift in the marriage, when the simple truth (if we accept it) is that it is not physically possible for men to do any of the above. After all, men can't breast-feed, can they?

Nor can they give birth. So, why harass them for something that is just not conceivable for them to do?

If you manage to cross the hurdle of the initial difficult months, however, this sense of irritation doesn't really last. Once you start feeling better, somewhere around the same time that the baby blows its first wet kiss at you and looks at you with wonder, round eyes following your every movement, everything else disappears and fades away. The only thing that remains is the miracle of having created a life together.

So, come on, ladies, let's not be unreasonable. Let us accept the fact that we need to—in fact, we have to—take on the primary responsibility of baby-making, and there is no point resenting our partners for something they are not physiologically able to do. And however much we may want to, we can't outsource this particular job. (I know we could, what with IVF and Aamir and Kiran doing the surrogate thing and all that, but you know what I mean.)

CORPORATE MANTRA OF THE DAY

- There comes a time in most women's lives when they need to take a break from their careers, short or long, to go through the process of childbearing. We need to take it in our stride and not resent our partners for not being able to play an equal role in the process.

PSST...

- The entire trauma is going to be finally worth it. I assure you that when you see the first toothy smile of your baby, you're not going to regret it.
- There are so many things you can blame guys for, why hassle them over things which they (or you) just cannot change?

8

WOMEN ONLY GET BETTER WITH AGE

AUNTYJI

Something happens to women when the march of time inexorably pushes them towards the age of forty. I have seen it happen to quite a few of my friends, who suddenly start behaving quite bizarrely from their thirty-ninth birthday onwards. And while the mid-life crisis, as undergone by men, has been widely documented in terms of the Harley-Davidsons they start buying, or the tattoos they start sprouting all over their bodies, or the affairs they start having with the closest twenty-six-year-old bimbette around, no one has talked about what happens to women at this age. So, it seems to me that we should spend some time analysing this phenomenon and figuring out the correct way for us to deal with this occurrence.

Typically, the first thing that women do is go on crash diets as they approach their tryst with forty. Having lost weight dramatically by following the latest fad diet (and having paid a bomb to the newest celebrity diet expert), they then go on shopping sprees and buy utterly unsuitable outfits (that they should have worn when they were twenty but were too conventional/scared to wear or couldn't afford to buy). They are now ready to party—and party hard!

With the determination and gusto of an engine whose brakes have failed, they embark on a social whirlwind. Obviously, no one has told them that they look like classy vultures, given the spindly legs and haggard faces their diet has reduced them too. (I tried saying this to a friend once and almost had my head immediately bitten off; I forgave her graciously and immediately when I realized that she had been surviving on lettuce leaves and puffed rice for the last fifteen days.) Clad in tiny frocks, they preen and primp and tell everyone how much weight they have lost, exhibiting their bony knees to all and sundry. (A fatal error, my dears. No one, except your truly devoted husband of twenty years, should be exposed to those knees.)

Now, I personally believe that except for the fashion police no one should have a problem if women at this age behave in any particular manner. And I do understand the issues that give rise to this behaviour—it is a kind of rebellion, a thumbing-your-nose type of revolt which has its roots in two things.

The first: when these women were growing up and had fine figures to display, there were not enough fashionable choices in apparel. (Remember, they were growing up when heroines used to either wear silk saris, oversized salwar suits or frilly frocks, all of which were not exactly created to display those curves—unless it was Silk Smitha, of course, in which case the curves immediately overpowered any outfit she wore.)

The second: post the age of thirty, women in India get unwillingly chucked into a 'past shelf life' corner by society.

Nothing defines this plunge into obscurity better than the ubiquitous 'Auntyji' label that gets applied to any lady above the age of twenty-eight. Everyone, from the postman to the grocery delivery boy to the next-door neighbour's pesky son, starts calling you 'Aunty' once you're beyond that age or married (whichever comes earlier) with an ease that suggests that they have been given the moral right to do so by society.

I promise you that no woman is particularly thrilled to be addressed thus. Like with Hindi film actresses who, post thirty, start getting offered mother-sister roles with the same male actors they were earlier paired with, this labelling suggests both insult and inequity in equal measure. The first time this happens, it creates a sense of shock and dismay in all women. And then, with every 'Aunty' call-out, their self-image keeps moving southwards, till it finally ends up like a limp rag somewhere near their ankles.

After nearly a decade of being called 'Aunty', I was so reconciled to the fact that I was middle-aged that when some roadside Romeo-type started whistling and making kissy-kissy sounds while following me down a deserted street in Chennai, I didn't even realize at first that I was being harassed. When it finally dawned on me, let me admit quite honestly that, just for a moment, I was somewhat flattered. (Here I was, thirty-five years of age, with ten years of being an aunty behind me, and someone was eve-teasing me. Wow!) In the next moment, of course, I walked across and gave him one tight slap as a matter of principle, since I strongly believe that every such lout should be given immediate feedback with a good thrashing. But my heart really wasn't in it.

So, do you now understand that if women do lose it a bit when they reach the ripe age of forty there is some justification to it? Protesting and screaming they have been willy-nilly dragged into the aunty corner much before their time, if they have now gathered the confidence to rebel, I say more power to them!

All my friends tell me that by the time they turn forty they develop a sense of self-confidence and a willingness to take the world head on, something they had been chary of doing so far. Up until then, they had either not been strong enough or too busy to stand up for themselves.

If you map the journey of a woman's life, you realize the truth of what they are saying. For example, being a teenager is so awkward for females. You are constantly feeling self-conscious and embarrassed about something or the other—your parents, the pimple on your forehead, the fact that you haven't worn the right outfit for the party, your chest developing too fast, or not quickly enough... You're perpetually living in a zone of extremes, either floating on air because the cute boy next door smiled at you, or in the depths of despair because your best friend did not return your call. It's all very difficult and uncomfortable.

When you reach your twenties, you are just trying too hard. Do you get invited to the most happening parties? Do you have the maximum number of fashionable clothes and boyfriends? Here, it's not about quality but quantity, so you shop from Palika Bazaar and Linking Road. Same principle when it comes to boyfriends and lifestyle—your self-esteem is defined by the number of bouquets you received on your birthday or the number of times you were able to party on weekdays or the number of tequila shots you could consume. A pretty insecure time all around.

In the thirties, you are now at middle-management level, with one kid and one husband in tow. Life is suddenly very busy and you are juggling being wife, mother, daughter and trying to rise up the corporate ladder, while paying two EMIs.

You are so harried and hassled that you don't even realize that the kid next door has started calling you 'Aunty'.

And then arrive the glorious forties. You have achieved a certain success and confidence. You know your strengths as a person and are pretty much satisfied with what you have. There's no need to prove anything to anyone any longer. You can wear, say and do what you want. If you have become slightly plump, you have the experience (and money) to invest in quality clothes which flatter you. With the children not requiring so much monitoring and the husband playing golf, you finally have lots of 'me-time', which you can use to do whatever you wish to do—spa, meditation class, party with friends, read, spend more time in office, start that new business you always dreamt of... There's an aura of poise and self-assurance about you that is very attractive. And, voila, you have morphed from aunty to cougar!

Let us then accept all the delightful things that happen to us as we mature. Like wine, we only become better with age. And the dollops of confidence that every passing year gives us ensures that we can openly demand and get a more equal part of the sky as our share—in our offices, our businesses and our homes! With plunging necklines, knobbly knees and oozing self-confidence, let us march on, not caring a whit of what the world thinks of us, and reach out for what some of us couldn't when we were younger and had more responsibilities and less courage.

CORPORATE MANTRA OF THE DAY

- As women grow older, their self-confidence and willingness to assert themselves increase. With fewer family responsibilities, they can now concentrate on themselves and look for what they truly want out of life.

- It is the best time for women to maximize their potential and do what they couldn't do when they were younger—whether it is learning pottery or starting a new business.

Psst...

- While I agree that you can do whatever you want and support you wholeheartedly, I sincerely urge you to accept that frocks and frills don't look good on mature women, however fashionable they may be. Avoid them, please.
- The confidence, style and experience emanating out of each pore now is immensely attractive to young men… Have fun, cougar lady!

9

WE CAN'T ALL BE SIZE ZERO

ARE CURVES IN OR OUT?

Women are late bloomers, as we just saw. Only as we grow older do we become more confident and assertive in our relationships. For a large part of our lives, we actually remain tentative and unsure of ourselves. Indeed, there are very few women I have met who accept themselves completely or are content with the way they are.

Specifically, in this era of size zero, I have yet to come across a single woman who has told me that she is happy with the way she looks. 'Shee, I am so overweight.' 'Uff, I hate my hips.' 'I wish I had a shorter nose.' 'I wish I was not so skinny.' (I abhor women who say this.) 'I like my right profile, but my left looks horrible, especially in the late afternoon light.' And, if everything is perfect, 'I do wish I had a dimple!'

However beautiful they are, there is always some flaw that women perceive in themselves. (I am told that Aishwarya absolutely detests the shape of her earlobes.) As a result, they are perpetually trying to change the way they appear. But while I have no complaints against superficial agents of improvement, like heels for height, creams for fairness, corsets to make-believe that we don't have hips (if we want to pretend we are closely related to the beanpole, so be it), I am unable to understand going under the scalpel or ingesting poison to make profound and permanent changes—cosmetic surgeries, tummy tucks, Botox. If not for any other reason but the simple fact that, like all things permanent, we can't go back or reverse the changes even if we want to—as an ex-actress of my acquaintance realized, much to her dismay.

Preeta Rai was an ex-beauty queen and one-film wonder anchoring a show for us, in the days when I used to head a lifestyle TV channel. It was supposed to be an Oprah equivalent with celebrity guests, heart-to-heart conversations with them, and high emotional quotient. Before you ask, Preeta Rai had been selected because of her 'contacts'—both in the celebrity world and the highest echelons of the organization which owned the lifestyle channel. So we had instructed the entire team to treat her with kid gloves.

In keeping with its theme, the chat show was supposed to have dollops of drama and emotion, with every third episode requiring the anchor and a large part of the audience to dissolve into sympathetic tears after listening to yet another story of suffering as narrated by the celebrity of the week. 'I slept on the pavement and begged at least a hundred producers for a role before I got my break.' 'My boyfriend asked me to do the item number as a favour, and then ditched me, otherwise I wanted to pick up only significant cinema roles.' You get the drift.

A fortnight after we had started shooting, I got a call from Preeta at 1 a.m. 'Darling, why haven't I seen you at the shoot so far?' she queried sulkily.

'Preeta, I have been busy with the launch plans for the channel. Hope all is well?' I said. I had heard things were not going too well on the sets but hadn't had time to figure out what exactly the problem was.

'Oh, the show is too marvellous, my dear, I am really enjoying being in front of the camera after so long, you know. And, of course, all the guests are personal friends, so it's no problem. But you must change your production team, darling, I insist.' I could hear her pouting at the other end of the phone.

'Why? I have put my best team to work with you, Preeta. I know that, being so professional yourself, you will want to work with only the finest.'

'Darling, they don't understand any lighting techniques, there are shadows all over my face, they are making me look positively ugly,' she wailed.

'Okay, okay, don't worry. I'll solve the problem,' I said soothingly. 'You go back to sleep now. We don't want any horrid dark circles under our eyes, do we?'

How did one explain to her that it was age—not the lighting—that was playing games with her?

However, Preeta's temper tantrums continued and, since the show was not evolving the way we had envisaged, I changed the entire production team (twice) and then the executive producer and then the writer. But everyone, including Preeta, could clearly see that the show was falling flat on its face. And none of us could figure out why till, finally, the director walked up to me one day and said, 'Boss, I want to show you something.' And he started playing some of the footage we had shot so far.

'And so my mom pulled me out of school and started doing the rounds of producers' offices when my father passed away...' sniffed a young starlet.

Cut to Preeta. Reaction shot. Preeta, with a fixed and frozen smile on her face: 'You poor thing!'

'The first producer, who gave me my break, came to my

vanity van at night, completely drunk...' continued the young starlet, tears rolling down her lovely face.

Cut to Preeta. Reaction shot. Preeta, with a fixed and frozen smile on her face: 'Oh, no, how horrible!'

'And when I objected, he threatened to throw me out of the film and tell the whole world I had tried to blackmail him and had taken money from him.' The starlet was in full flow now.

Cut to Preeta. Reaction shot. Preeta, with a fixed and frozen smile on her face: 'Oh my God! What a sleazeball!'

'You see what's happening?' The director groaned. 'She is just not able to give any good reaction shots in response. Her face is just so numb. Otherwise, with these stories, what a show I could have given you! What TRPs!' And he started banging his head against the nearest wall.

'But why?' I was puzzled. 'I seem to remember she wasn't such a bad actress. What's happened to her now?'

'Oh, that's because she's been Botoxed. All her facial muscles have frozen up!' snickered the young EP standing next to us.

Poor Preeta! So that was the reason why the show was not working. We had an ice queen as anchor when what we needed was a drama queen.

We finally had to get rid of her and withdraw the show.

Preeta had tried to hold on to her youth, but in the bargain had lost the ability to emote. And the irony was that we would have been happy to have her, wrinkles and all, as long as she could have given us some strong emotional interplay and sensitive drama with the guests and the audience.

Like Preeta, many women today are cutting, poisoning and starving themselves in a bid to transform into what they believe is an ideal and beautiful woman and, in the process, losing all their individuality and emerging as clones of the latest diva.

At first, ever since Kareena showed us how, we all started trying to get as close to size zero as possible. And just as we had finally figured out how to reach single digit sizes, the concept of beauty changed—as one of my skinny friends realized when she was gently told by her husband that it would be a good idea for her to put on some weight and display some curves. Coincidentally, this conversation happened a few minutes after they had watched *The Dirty Picture*.

With Vidya B becoming the pin-up girl for all males between eight and eighty, the tables turned overnight and curves were suddenly back in fashion. Men cannily started bringing desserts home for their wives and girlfriends. (Much like my uncle from Amritsar used to do, where apparently it is the norm for husbands to carry a little offering for their wives every day when they return from work, otherwise the door does not get opened.) Indeed, men begun actively encouraging their better halves to give up following various diets and get back to the original hearty Punju or Gujju meal plan propounded by their mothers instead.

From modelling themselves on anorexic Anoushka, women now had to quickly morph into voluptuous Vidyas, if they wanted to be contemporary in their looks. Having forgotten how to eat, the poor things found it difficult to swallow anything wider than a bread stick. After years of counting every calorie and positive and negative PUFA and MUFA that was put on their plates, they couldn't figure out how to cope with this dilemma of plenty. With tears rolling down their cheeks, many of them were now eating rasagollas and gulabjamuns, tasting them for the first time ever.

In contrast to these fad-followers, there are people like Usha Uthup, the renowned singer, for example. So cool and so comfortable in her own skin! With that superlative husky voice and the kind of songs she sings, if she had been trying to live up to the world's image of what a Western music performer should look like, she would have been desperately trying to fit into a tiny black cocktail dress meant for teenagers. Whereas, here she is, looking as if she is from a khata-peeta household, as we say in our Punjab, wearing Kanjivaram saris, with flowers in her hair and matching sneakers to boot. A style uniquely her own. What self-belief, what innate poise—and what a joy to see and hear her!

Truly, women like her are worthy icons to emulate, not in the letter but in the spirit of the confident individuality they portray, rather than blind adulation of some perfect concept of beauty which has (in most cases) been programmed into our minds by men. Let us learn to accept and love ourselves as we are. I promise, shorn of all the external pressure, we will come to the conclusion that we are largely fine just the way we are. And then, with only a minor tweak here and there, a little powder, a spot of lipstick, some spit and a bit of polish, we will realize we are more than good to go!

CORPORATE MANTRA OF THE DAY

- We all have unique personalities of our own; why can't we showcase that in the way we appear rather than follow the latest trends?
- Style comes from the substance which is already within each one of us. Being comfortable in your own skin is the best sign of confidence and self-esteem.

PSST...

- Look before you leap. You may regret some of the permanent changes you are making to your body right now, like tattooing the initials of your current boyfriend or freezing up your facial muscles.

10

THE ENEMY IS WITHIN

RANI OR RAKSHASINI?

So, is the myth that it's mostly women who are responsible for other women's misery true, or is it just a story? Or is it some devious divide-and-rule game being played by men? Or maybe blaming other women for our difficulties is nothing but some kind of externalizing we are indulging in...

I was discussing this with two women friends who run a successful business. Both were vehement in their opinion that other women had been largely obstructive when they were trying to build their business in the initial years, and it was their male associates who truly helped them.

A possible theory here is that till a few years ago there were fewer women in the work environment, and the ones who were there were benefactors of the tokenism that prevailed in organizations in those days, that of hiring women to fulfil some kind of quota. As a consequence, in a bid to protect their turf and their 'reserved seats', they didn't want other women to succeed.

However, today it has become a fairly even playing field; if are competing, it is as much with your male colleagues as your female ones. As such, if you have to be hostile and unhelpful, you will be so with both. Of course, this is only a theory to answer the advocates of the 'woman against woman' myth.

Personally, I am not a subscriber to this viewpoint at all. I have interacted at work with scores of women, including two women bosses, and most of these interactions have been largely supportive and constructive. Malini, for example, was one of the most understanding bosses I have ever had. She worked very hard to mentor her women subordinates and actually fought with the management to change the policies in our organization and give people like me flexi-timing and other benefits during pregnancy.

While Malini was great, the other woman boss I had was a very difficult one indeed. Rekha Ma'am, as we called her, was pretty much universal in her toughness, reducing all her subordinates (male and female) to blithering idiots with her sarcasm infested tongue-lashings. Though, to be fair, many times they deserved what she doled out.

'Kavya, I am leaving now, and I expect you and Apurva to finish this magazine readership plan today and present it to me first thing tomorrow morning, do you understand?' Rekha barked out these instructions as she collected her car keys, cigarette case and lunch box, en route to her meeting at HQ one day.

'Yes, Rekha, we will be ready.' Kavya nodded her head vigorously while winking at me behind Rekha's back.

Shit, I thought to myself, what was Kavya up to now? She was certain to land me in trouble. She was in shit-street with Rekha already, now it would be my turn.

It was my first job and I had been assigned to Rekha's team at the end of the mandatory training programme for management trainees, and Kavya was my immediate reporting manager. Unfortunately, Rekha had decided that Kavya was a complete fool and had taken it upon herself to verbally annihilate her every morning and then stamp her into nothingness as a sort of life lesson to all of us juniors: 'See how idiots will be treated here.'

Thus, every morning would start off with a very public demonstration of this mission for us to see and learn from. (I think the canteen boy had actually started doling out tickets for the matinee, promising the audience a sizzling show full of action and drama.)

A fairly innocuous day would start off with Rekha bustling in with flashing eyes, heaving bosom and uneven temper. The entire office would hold its collective breath. After making herself a cup of coffee, she would settle in her chair, look at Kavya disapprovingly and start firing questions about all the tasks that had been assigned to her. Invariably, Kavya would have done half of them and would have either forgotten to do the balance or got them completely wrong. And that would set Rekha off on an orgy of raging and ranting, avidly watched by everyone, while Kavya's role was to stand and look penitent and, once in a while, plaintively bleat: 'But, Rekha...' Fuelled by a litre of hot rasam for breakfast (Rekha was a good South Indian), that tirade would be stopped by nothing. An hour or so of venting her spleen later, Rekha would storm off and Kavya would fall back like a limp rag on her desk.

Throughout the daily lashings, Kavya remained incorrigibly unchanged and would bounce back like an India-rubber ball, only to be quashed once again the next day—while I was so terrified of Rekha that I actually burst into tears when our GM assigned me to work with her after my training.

Anyway, as soon as Rekha left that day, I pounced on Kavya. 'Come on, let's hurry up and do the plan. It will take at least a couple of hours, I think.'

'Wait, sweetheart, I have to go for a Page 3 party and need a designer outfit for it. Let me organize that, and then we will get down to business,' she drawled.

Kavya then determinedly got to the task of dialling all her model friends to borrow the aforementioned garment. Unfortunately, it proved to be more elusive than she had thought; by the time she managed to get hold of it, it was almost time for her to leave. By now, I was climbing up the wall in terror, reduced to a gibbering idiot imagining Rekha's face the next day when she realized we had no plan to show her.

'Relax, dear, Mama Kavya has everything under control.' Kavya patted my shoulder.

'Under control?' I squeaked. 'You are leaving in ten minutes and we haven't done any analysis so far. I haven't ever done a media plan in my life, so I can't do one on my own, and Rekha will kill us... Oh, God, what are we going to do, eeee...' I wailed.

For the life of me, I couldn't understand how Kavya could look so calm. All that shouting every morning, had she secretly started enjoying it? Was she into S&M? Or had she poisoned the last cup of coffee she had brought for Rekha and knew she would not be coming to office the next day? My mind started running around in circles trying to figure out why she was so cool and collected. I was just one notch short of full-blown hysteria.

'What are you doing?' I stared goggle-eyed at Kavya when I saw her pull out the previous year's plan and start to make copies.

'I told you not to worry,' she smirked.

'But we can't use that, it's cheating,' I whispered.

'Oh, don't be such a baby. All you management trainee types, so pure and noble! Grow up, babe. In any case, nothing much has changed in magazine readership, she won't make out the difference.' With that, Kavya sauntered off to her party.

Obviously, I didn't sleep a wink that night and contemplated jumping before the tracks at least twice on my way to work the next day. Come 11 a.m., the door opened and in walked Rekha.

She was wearing a black sari. I groaned—we all knew that her moods always matched the colour of her outfits. Of course, in the two months I had been around, I had not seen her in anything except red, purple and dark blue, so I couldn't really imagine her having a sunny yellow or a soothing blue mood—though I had been told that, once in a while, when her chakras were all aligned, it did happen.

'Please show me the plan.' She smiled (maliciously, I thought) at Kavya.

Did she know? Her left eyebrow was twitching, and that evil sneer... I was ready to puke in fright.

Rekha glanced at the plan, flicking her fingers disdainfully through the sheets. 'Why have you chosen *Femina* instead of *Filmfare* to advertise in?'

'Err, we decided to do that because we have also taken *Movie* magazine and the duplication of readers between *Filmfare* and *Movie* is very high,' responded Kavya.

'Oh, is that right? And what exactly is the duplication between *Femina* and *Movie*?' Rekha asked.

'I don't remember off-hand, but I can go look up the calculations if you want,' said Kavya bravely.

'Please do so. Or, wait, why don't you bring the calculations here so we can all look at them together?' Rekha countered. And Kavya was sent off to fetch her claimed calculations.

Rekha glared at me. 'She's lying, isn't she? This is last year's plan, right? And there are no calculations?' Her eyes pierced into me, probing every nook and cranny of my mind.

I didn't know what to say; agreeing with her would have branded me a snitch and replying in the negative a liar. I promptly did what I was getting very good at doing in her vicinity—I burst into copious tears.

And then, Rekha brought out her full artillery and launched into Kavya with such a blistering attack that, twenty years later, I still get the quakes when I think about it!

Kavya obviously didn't last too long after that episode, but she ensured that she badmouthed Rekha to everyone she could and branded her a bitch suffering from perpetual PMS to all and sundry.

To many people who don't even know her, Rekha will always be a horrible woman who was unnecessarily aggressive and who didn't support the sisterhood, given that she was so harsh with women subordinates—while the truth is that she was equally tough with male juniors, especially when they deserved it. Thanks to Kavya, she became yet another illustration of the 'It's women who pull other women down' myth and will forever get clubbed with sisters-in-law and mothers-in-law as impediments in the cause of female empowerment. When the reality was so different!

Blaming other women is nothing but yet another form of externalizing our problems. The fact is that the enemy is within us! The decision to leave jobs and give up at the first sign of a problem or run away from a tough boss or tough project—or not even take the trouble to work hard, like Kavya—is a choice we make and not one that is forced on us by anyone outside.

Many a time, we delude ourselves into thinking that other women, whether they are unsupportive female colleagues, difficult mothers-in-law or conservative mothers, are the reason for some of the less courageous decisions we have taken, when clearly the choice has been made by the weakness, the lack of motivation and the unwillingness to fight that is within us.

And hence the last lesson in this particular segment for all of us is to look not for the enemy outside of us but accept that often she is within us—and then learn to deal with her.

CORPORATE MANTRA OF THE DAY

- 'Women are nasty to other women' is a myth we need to debunk immediately.
- We need to understand that the enemy could be our internal demons and learn to deal with them first.

PSST...

- If we keep blaming the Rekhas around us for all our shortcomings, when will we learn to deal with them ourselves? Our mothers-in-law and female bosses can be scapegoats for only so long.

THE TEN LESSONS OF ACCEPTANCE

1. **I accept my femininity**

   We don't have to apologize for being women; we must accept all our feminine traits unreservedly. Thankfully, there is no longer any need to behave and look like a man to succeed.

2. **I accept that I will feel guilty**

   Every woman has the right to choose to be either a working mom or a stay-at-home mom or not a mom at all. However, in all cases, there will be some guilt attached. We have to accept that guilt comes along as part of the territory of being a woman.

3. **I accept that life is unfair—not only to women but to men too**

   While it may seem that life has been unjust largely to women, the fact is that men too have many challenges they face, including having to live up to the stereotype of being the main provider of the family.

4. **I accept that I can multitask and thus will end up doing more work**

   Multitasking is a unique skill which only women appear to have; we should accept it as our strength and not as a burden, and use it to the fullest capacity to move ahead in the race.

5. **I accept that being a masochistic sufferer is simply not cool**

   In today's day and age, suffering is no longer seen as

noble but downright impractical and foolish. So let us stop playing the martyr's role.

6. I accept that I have to wait patiently to take over the world

Traditional stereotypes are slowly blurring and both genders are borrowing characteristics from each another. Men will have to morph into women if they want to survive in the new world; we simply need to be patient.

7. I accept that men can't bear children

There comes a time in most women's lives when we will have to take a break from our careers to go through the process of childbearing. We need to take it in our stride and not resent our partners for not being able to play an equal role in the process.

8. I accept that I will improve with age

As women grow older, we become more confident. It is then the best time for us to maximize our potential and do what we couldn't do when we were younger— whether it is to learn pottery or start a new business.

9. I accept that everyone need not be size zero

Women need to love themselves just the way they are. Each of us has a unique personality which should form the basis of our individual self-worth.

10. I accept that I can be my own worst enemy

'Women are nasty to other women' is a myth we all need to debunk and accept the fact that many times we ourselves are the cause of our own problems.

PART II

ADAPTING

Adapt yourself to your reality—and then you will be able to mould reality to what you want.

11

THE RIGHT ATTITUDE IS THE STARTING POINT

HAVING A POSITIVE MINDSET

Do you remember the beautiful patterns the kaleidoscope used to make when you peered through the peephole and shook it? Lovely multicoloured designs and gorgeous configurations, each more delightful than the other. As kids, we spent hours simply admiring them. Even though, when you actually think about it, the components were nothing but shards of glass.

In my more fanciful moments, I think our lives are a lot like that: parts of it are only individual pieces of coloured glass, but put together we can create a beautiful design.

The second leg of our journey, which is of learning how to adapt to the realities around us, is pretty much like that. It is the stage when we pick up all the facts that we learnt to accept in stage one, make them work in our favour rather than against us, and create a unique and beautiful pattern of achievement of our own.

Since the starting point of any endeavour lies within us, if we have to learn to modify ourselves and our environment to suit our needs, the foremost thing to do is to start off with a positive mindset. So, step one in adapting is winning the battle in our minds.

I studied for my graduation at Stella Maris College in Chennai, one of the finest institutions of learning in South India. While it purported to be a senior college, it had a very rigid and convent school-like atmosphere, with strict rules and regulations, including locking the gates of the college during working hours (both to keep the girls in and the boys out) and sending us home if we dared to wear short skirts or sleeveless blouses. (I still haven't been able to figure out why this last rule was in force, since the only two males I ever saw on campus in my three years there were the ninety-seven-year-old gardener and the partially blind guard at the entrance.)

While our souls were being ritually cleansed and purified by moral science classes every morning and our minds vigorously enlightened through a tough study schedule, the college also actively encouraged our physical development with a very correct and high-minded 'body is the temple of the soul' attitude. As such, willingly or unwillingly, all of us had to sign up for a sport the moment we entered the hallowed portals of the college. Serendipitously, I joined the hockey coaching sessions and, much to everyone's surprise (including mine), ended up getting selected to be part of the college team. To everyone's further surprise and shock, my short sporting career graph rose sharply and dramatically with my selection to play as goalkeeper for Madras University and subsequently for the Tamil Nadu state team.

My entire circle of family and friends was taken aback by this hitherto unexhibited talent, having witnessed a distinct disinclination on my part to move very much from my favourite armchair; I, on the other hand, was quite surprised by the fact that I ended up enjoying the sport very much. The early morning practice sessions, the gut-wrenching sit-ups, the straps chafing into ankles, the blue bruises all over our legs—everything paled into insignificance compared to the camaraderie of the team, the satisfying thwack of the ball into the opponent team's goalpost and the glory of various saves made with courageous leaps at the ball.

The Tamil Nadu Women's Hockey Team comprised a motley group of girls from all parts of the state—from sophisticated Chennai to gauche North Arcot and Salem—and one of the first tournaments we participated in was the All India National Women's Annual Sports Meet held in Punjab that year. In our little corner of the world in Tamil Nadu, we had been the stars of the hockey fraternity; however, we soon realized that the national meet was a different ballgame altogether, and we were no match for the strapping players from Punjab, the hardy Haryanvis, or the quicksilver teams of the North East. We lost the first two matches in quick succession and by a wide margin (the scores were more like basketball scores than hockey ones—12-0 and 7-0), and it was rare for the ball to even cross into the opponents' side of the field.

Finally, the morning of our third and last game dawned. Frankly speaking, many of us were looking forward to packing our bags and disappearing from the scene of our ignominious defeats as quickly as possible. As the goalkeeper of the team, I believed that I was culpable for the losses and was convinced that I would be dropped from the next game, not realizing that it was the entire team and not just me who had been thoroughly outclassed by our opponents.

The coach gathered all of us around her at the start of the warm-up session and, with a hearty smile on her face, chivvied us: 'Courage, girls. This is an easier match, and I want all of you to forget what has happened so far. Play like you have always played back home. Let's give them a tough fight!'

Taking her words to heart, all the girls determinedly started their warm-up routine, dribbling the ball, practising passes and exercising their muscles. I, however, just stood in a corner, moping. Sheryl, our captain, ran up to me and whispered furiously: 'What the hell are you doing? Come on, get on the field quickly. Do you want to be dropped from the team?' Loath to ignore her, I started warming up in a desultory fashion and with a complete lack of enthusiasm. The coach was watching all this with an eagle eye. When the time came to announce the eleven who would play the match, she dropped me and asked the back-up goalkeeper to pad up and go on to the field. The team played bravely, but we lost that match too.

The coach walked up to me later on. 'What was going on before the match? I hope you realize I dropped you not because you were playing badly but because I could not afford to have a goalkeeper who had lost even the desire to try to win. I needed eleven determined players out there, not ten!'

It was then that realization dawned: it was not losing the earlier games but my negativity and unwillingness to try that had determined whether I would be part of the team or not. Through my demeanour, I had clearly indicated to the coach that in my mind I had already lost the game before even stepping on the field; and, as coach, her duty was to play a team which was willing to at least make an effort till the final whistle, even if the odds were clearly stacked against us.

This happened nearly twenty-five years ago, but I have never forgotten the lesson I learnt on that cold winter morning on the hockey field in Chandigarh. I learnt that in life one has to keep trying ceaselessly and continuously in whatever one undertakes. Oftentimes, there will be things that will not go our way, but we have to keep pushing, striving and trying. Unfortunately, many times, when the going gets tough, the first battle we lose is the one in our mind. We start creating mental ghosts and presupposing the worst.

'I will not feel a part of the team since I am the only female.' 'I will lose my job if I ask for flexi timings.' 'My boss hates me.' 'This project will be taken away from me if I tell them I am pregnant.' 'I only have bad luck, I have no one to help me at work or at home.' When we say these things, the ghosts in our minds become concrete truths for us and more tangible than the reality, which could be completely different. It is our own negativity that prevents us from trying to overcome the challenges in front of us.

As the hockey story demonstrates, our poor attitude becomes the first step we take towards self-inflicted failure, pushed into that direction only by our own mindset. Whereas, starting with a positive mindset can change things around and actually propel us towards success.

CORPORATE MANTRA OF THE DAY

- Everyone faces obstacles in life. People who succeed are those who approach these problems with a positive mindset.
- Most wars are lost in our minds much before we have stepped out on the battlefield.

PSST...

- In a choice between skill and great attitude, attitude always wins, hands down.
- Bosses like people who are cheerleaders, who are willing to try, who want to find solutions. A good way to be knocked off a team is to be the one who always shows everyone the pitfalls.

12

NOBODY'S YET FOUND A SUBSTITUTE FOR HARD WORK

EXPECTANT EXPECTATIONS!

Prateeka, one of our finance executives, walked up to me one day with a box of sweets. 'Ma'am, I want to share some good news with you. I am pregnant,' she said coyly.

'Congratulations, Prateeka! But I thought you just got married? Fast work, huh?' I quizzed gently.

We all burst into laughter as she blurted out: 'Yes, ma'am, but I don't know how it happened.'

Prateeka had joined the company a few months ago and, initially, with her hard work and diligence, proven to be an asset to the team. However, within two months of coming on board, she applied for leave to get married, which we had agreed to reluctantly. And now she was all set to go on maternity leave, within a year of becoming part of the organization.

As a diversity conscious organization, we had no choice but to work within the constraints of her needs, but I could understand the angst of the HOD who would be working with one member less for the better part of the year. Especially given the small teams all of us operate with, in a tightened economic environment, one member pulling less weight can cause a big loss of efficiency within a department.

We decided to make the best of the situation and manage as well as we could. A few weeks later, I noticed that while the entire finance team was working late hours every day to complete the quarterly audit Prateeka was missing from the scene completely. The next time I saw her, I queried: 'Where have you been, Prateeka? I haven't seen you around.'

She looked at me in round-eyed amazement. 'But I told you, ma'am, I am pregnant.'

'Yes, I know that. But what does that have to do with not coming to office or leaving early, which I am told you are doing regularly?' I persisted, irritated by her astonishment. 'I assume everything is okay, health-wise, and the doctor has given you a clean chit to travel and work?'

'Yes, ma'am. But I have been feeling a bit giddy and nauseous lately, so I decided to rest for a few days. And my husband is so worried about me, he absolutely forbade me from travelling...' she trailed off, apparently peeved that I was questioning her about work when her expectant state required tender pampering instead.

And throughout her pregnancy, we had to deal with Prateeka's giddiness, her morning sickness, her husband's concern, her mother's anxiety, her grandmother's opinion on when she should work and when she should rest, and so on.

In contrast, when Amrita, a dear friend and colleague, was going through her pregnancy, it was very much business and work as usual. She travelled every single day, first by bus, then hour-long by train, then fifteen minutes of walking to reach office. She did that for almost eight months of her pregnancy, barely missing a day in all that while. And poor

Amrita didn't just have morning sickness—she had morning, afternoon and evening sickness that she dealt with valiantly, carrying plastic bags with her wherever she went, including to client meetings. At one meeting, she had to excuse herself in the middle of a presentation, go and deal with her sickness and come back while all of us carried on with our discussions, taking the interruption as par for the course. (The client, as it happened, was a recent father himself and empathized with us.) On one of the occasions when she was really ill and the doctor forced her to rest at home for a couple of days, Amrita actually lay in bed and completed a host of calculations I needed for an urgent review.

All of us have worked hard, travelled across the city by public transport, stood in queues wherever required, treating our pregnancies as just another part of life, neither expecting nor getting any special treatment from anyone around us (except our families, of course). At times, while I stood with an aching back all the way on the return journey from work during my pregnancy, I would wonder why no one in the ladies' compartment got up and offered me her seat. But then I realized that, like me, most of the women around had surely made the journey in the same state themselves some time or the other, matter-of-fact-ly dealing with the shoves and pushes of a Mumbai train, getting no latitude from any of the harried commuters around them. They obviously expected everyone else to be able to handle the same too.

Especially, and rather unfortunately, at the stage when they have children, many bright women give up because balancing a career and a family and kids requires tremendous hard work and effort. It's like having two jobs for at least fifteen years of your life, constantly juggling two shifts, each with their own pulls, pressures and demands. It's not getting a Sunday lie-in with breakfast in bed, except once a year on your birthday; it's forgetting about the all-night partying that was a weekly affair once upon a lifetime ago; it's about a daily task list about thirty-five chores long, ranging from 'validate the compliance checklist' to 'get little coloured stones for the EVED school project'. (Since I was informed about this by Sid at approximately 10.30 p.m. the night before the submission, I actually went down to the roadside and picked up tiny gravel stones and spent half the night painting them in different colours.)

Working hard and persevering at every stage in our lives is a non-negotiable factor if we want to succeed. As someone once said, 'It's amazing that the more I work the luckier I get!'

It's certainly not for the faint-hearted, this entire process of being mummy, wife and ideal employee. But if one persists diligently, all the hard work does pay off and ultimately translates into success.

Corporate mantra of the day

- The single most important driver of success in life is perseverance. And women who have succeeded have done so only because they simply didn't give up, just like the ant who keeps trying again and again to take that piece of grain up the mound.
- Running away from hard work is running away from success; do so at your own peril.

Psst...

- Pregnancy is not an illness, it's a process of life. Don't use it as an excuse to shirk your responsibilities at work.
- Your boss is not your mother; get all the mollycoddling you want at home. Be a true professional and don't expect indulgence at work.

13

LEARNING TO PRIORITIZE

IS THAT A BIRD? IS THAT A PLANE? NO, IT'S SUPERWOMAN!

As we discussed in the previous chapter, working hard is mandatory for women who want to make a success of both their professional and personal lives. However, a key factor that ensures all that hard work translates into success is also working 'smart' by learning to prioritize within that workload.

If anyone out there believes that she can be a great hostess, a superlative cook and an exemplary employee, while simultaneously attending all the PTA meetings, chairing the school's Christmas pageant, learning scuba-diving and attending every possible industry forum, let me assure her, poor child, that she is deluding herself. It's not going to happen.

However hardworking and clever you are, if you try and juggle all the balls that are thrown at you, some of them will definitely fall down and break. You simply have to learn to let go of some of the dispensable stuff and be content with doing only a few things at a time, and doing them really well, in order to attain results.

This prioritizing requires figuring out how to separate the essential tasks from the inessential ones and learning to focus on relevant responsibilities and either ignoring—or, better still—delegating the irrelevant ones. (For years, I have been delegating meal preparation—which I hate and consider irrelevant—to mother, cook, husband and, now, my son, who is turning out to be an awesome cook.) At various stages in our lives and careers, these priorities will not remain constant but change; it is important to choose only a few which are critical at each juncture and focus on just them.

Sheila, for instance, is very clear that her first priorities today are the small catering business she manages, her two growing kids and her family. Known as Eveready Sheila in her younger days, she was the one all of us could rely on should we need a last-minute partner to a corporate party, a companion to attend a boring wedding, a friend to impetuously take an unscheduled weekend break with, or just someone to go driving halfway to Lonavala at 2 a.m. on a whim! However, today, none of us can recognize her in her current avatar, of responsible entrepreneur and mom. Her life runs like clockwork, with every hour scheduled and accounted for weeks in advance. She is totally focused on the quality of output in her business and her children's activities and studies, and she is doing a wonderful job of both.

I asked her one day if she regretted not having the freedom to do anything impulsively any longer. Her answer was very simple: 'I think there is a time and place for everything in life. There is a time to be irresponsible and there is a time to take care of something or someone. Priorities need to change at different stages of our life if we want to grow and evolve.'

Similarly, Ananya took a conscious call to delay having a

baby so that she could concentrate on her job at an MNC during the initial hectic years of the start of its operations in the country.

These are examples of milestones that occur once in a blue moon and require deep thinking (and severe heartburn) before we make our choices; however, prioritizing is more often a daily affair in most of our lives and involves the small choices we have to make every single day. Boss's house for a drink, or home to help son finish his homework? Husband's office party, or the late-evening department meeting? Half-day off to make home-cooked lunch for relatives during Durga puja, or finishing the appraisals on schedule?

Enough women have burnt themselves out in attempting to be Superwoman, trying to do every task themselves and trying to excel at everything. Running around in circles in a bid to be perfect can result in huge stress, and a day will come when you snap under pressure and just give up. Why reach that stage when a little letting go of the desire to be perfect could lead to staying on course in the marathon that is the life of a working woman? It's okay not to be able to cook a gourmet meal, or to miss out on a couple of sports meets, or to not have all the answers to the client's queries at the tip of your fingers once in a while.

I bumped into Vibha at the mall one day. She looked flustered and out of sorts. 'What's the problem, Vibha?'

'Oh, hi, nothing, nothing at all,' she said in a distracted fashion, continuing to look through the shelves, picking up and discarding one box of serviettes after another.

'Can I help? What are you searching for?'

'I want pink serviettes, and they only have yellow or white ones,' she muttered.

'Any particular reason you are looking for pink?' I asked, puzzled by such a specific requirement.

'To go with the pink roses in my centrepiece, of course. I'm having a party at home tonight for Harish's colleagues.' She looked at me as if I had asked a particularly silly question. 'I think I'll hop across to the mall on MG Road, maybe they'll have that colour.' And off she whizzed.

Vibha has always been a whizzer. Unvaryingly and constantly, she whizzes from one thing to another at supersonic speed. She whizzes at work and she whizzes at home. I have known her for several years and I have never ever seen her calm or relaxed or staying still in one place for more than five minutes. A high achiever with a very competitive nature, she wants to be perfect in everything she does. So she whizzes around trying to be the best at her job, at cooking, at the parties she throws. Her daughter has to get the best grades in school and her husband the best increment.

For many years, she managed to sustain this achievement orientation and did remarkably well too. But then came the day of the Great Meltdown (the very same day that I had bumped into her at the mall)—a friend who was at Vibha's party later told me about it.

Everything was going perfectly till the dessert was brought out. Up until then, they had had finger-licking starters (not that finger licking was required, given the pink serviettes being handed out with every entrée, which perfectly matched the drinks that were served). The house sparkled, the staff was courteous and attentive, the food delicious and the music just right. Unfortunately, the tiramisu soufflé, which is supposed to be Vibha's specialty and her great pride and joy, turned out to be a disaster. Harish's boss had barely taken the first bite when he and everyone around realized that there was something drastically wrong—it had gone bad. No one knows quite how it happened, but the effect on Vibha was cataclysmic. She was so devastated that she got an anxiety attack and a doctor had to be brought in to give her a sedative.

Last I heard, Vibha had to take a sabbatical from work and go on a long holiday in the bracing air of a Himalayan mountain retreat to calm her nerves.

Unfortunately, many a time, high achievers are just not able to deal with failure of any kind. It doesn't matter how big or small it is, but failure per se is unacceptable to them.

One of my aunts was exactly the same. Having excelled at everything from an early age, she had an inflated opinion of herself and had set unreasonable benchmarks for all her family. They had to be perfect in everything, and she had to be better than everyone around her. And then, one day, as happens to all of us, she had to face disappointment. She didn't get a coveted promotion that she had been expecting. She had been sure of getting it—after all, she was the best manager the organization had ever seen. She was so shocked by this one failure that she could not bring herself to understand and work on the reasons behind being overlooked for the promotion, or even try and overcome the disappointment by focusing on other aspects of her largely happy life. Unwilling to be seen as anything less than excellent, she resigned and has never gone back to corporate life again. What a waste of talent, I always think.

My aunt has now withdrawn herself from anything that she can't control and lives in isolation in a perfectly kept mansion, growing perfect flowers and vegetables in a perfectly maintained garden. However, her competitive spirit still comes to the fore, and she intermittently gets in touch with us to let us know how she is living a perfect life, growing the best roses or tomatoes or spinach in the world. She has chosen not to be part of normal life because reality can be arbitrary and random.

Reality has disillusionments strewn along its path, which nobody can stop or control. But if you withdraw from it because of what you perceive as a 'significant' failure, you are also losing out on partaking of the richness and variety a fuller yet less perfect life can offer you, and the many triumphs (even if less 'significant') that can come your way.

CORPORATE MANTRA OF THE DAY

- Being able to prioritize what is important and what is not is a key skill for success.
- You don't need to be perfect; it is better to be outstandingly great at the specific areas you have chosen to focus on.

PSST...

- Pick up the things you really enjoy and excel in those. Delegate the rest.
- Accepting your limitations is character-building. Once in a while, compliment yourself for not being good at something—it helps you face reality and will hold you in good stead in the long run.

14

ASKING FOR HELP

CAN YOU GIVE UP CONTROL?

'Mummyji, I have made the ragi porridge for Sagar, will you feed him when he gets up? I am getting late for work. And then he has to be given a bath at 10 a.m. exactly. I have left the thermometer in the bathroom to check the water's temperature. And will you please remember to use the baby powder and not the normal one? I think his rash is an allergic reaction to that powder and...' recited Anju as she raced towards the door.

'Uff, Beta, why are you getting hassled? Don't worry, I will manage. You leave, you are already very late.' With that, my aunt shut the door decisively behind her daughter-in-law's retreating back. She shot me an annoyed look. 'Look at the way Anju goes on. As if Sagar is the first baby I am bringing up. I brought up three children with zero help. And see how well they have turned out...' She picked up the spoon to taste the aforementioned porridge. 'Yuck, no sugar. How will the poor child eat this, I ask you?' She added a generous spoonful of sugar to the ragi porridge.

'But Anju specifically asked you not to give Sagar sugar, didn't she, Aunty?' I reminded her.

'And where will that poor child get any energy? No sugar indeed! God knows what kind of newfangled ideas these girls pick up from the Internet these days. Have you tasted this stuff? My poor jaan didn't eat even a tiny bite yesterday till I added sugar to it. If the Good Lord hadn't meant us to eat it, he wouldn't have made sugar, no? I have brought up all your cousins with no problems by giving them everything to eat. And even you—did your mother deprive you like this when you were growing up, huh?' She glared at me.

I had been staying with my cousin and his wife for the last few days and had been watching—up, close and personal—the saas-bahu saga unfold between my aunt and Anju, much like a daily television soap drama with a new twist every day. Having lived amicably with each other for several years, my aunt and her daughter-in-law were normally close buddies; but they just could not see eye-to-eye on the upbringing of Sagar. So, each day would begin with Anju leaving detailed instructions about Sagar's routine with her mother-in-law and, while Aunty would not directly oppose her, as soon as she left she would do precisely what she thought was best for her grandson—whether it was feeding him sugar or letting him crawl in the little garden outside or giving him a massage with ghee rather than the special baby oil Anju had asked her sister to get from abroad. Aunty pretty much ignored Anju's every instruction and did what she pleased. It was, in a way, amusing to see Anju going to hysterical lengths to sterilize everything that Sagar used, including his bath tub and the mixer in which his porridge was made, while Aunty unperturbedly let the much-sanitized child put mud in his mouth as he played in the garden. She'd just calmly wash his face and then let him get back to crawling furiously in the grass.

Obviously, whenever Anju cottoned on to any of Aunty's shenanigans, there would be much heartburn and she would have a fit, heaping all her frustrations on my poor cousin, but she knew she couldn't do anything beyond that. She needed Aunty's help if she wanted to continue working, and she could see Sagar was flourishing under his grandmother's care, however unhygienic she may deem it.

If you analyse deeply, this is a key reason why many women don't ask for help when they are trying to manage home and work together. Not because they won't get it but because it often means loss of control—over rearing their children, of the kitchen, over the way they want to live their lives.

But the truth is that many times we do need support, from our families, our mothers, our mothers-in-law, as well as our organizations. If I hadn't asked the company where I worked twenty years ago if I could do flexi-timing, when diversity consciousness was still an unknown concept, I probably wouldn't be in this position today. And if my mother hadn't taken the entire responsibility of bringing up my son, I wouldn't have been able to keep up with the high-pressure job of running a TV channel. Yes, at times it does result in handing over charge of a precious part of your life to someone else. But especially in the case of rearing children, I think it makes far more sense to let your mother or mother-in-law into your space rather than some indifferent (though antiseptic!) day-care facility.

Women who seem to be managing a high-pressure job and a family with ease and savoir faire definitely ask for help. They create support systems around them—mother, neighbours, husband, household help—and use them extensively.

A few chapters back, we agreed that we would junk the Suffering Sita role model; therefore, in our newfound enlightened and emancipated avatars, there is nothing wrong in asking the rest of the household to pull its weight too. After all, if you are underwriting part of the financial inflow into the family, why should the rest of the family not contribute in the daily chores to keep home and hearth well-oiled and running? Ask your husband and children to help, but without demarcating responsibilities according to gender. Girls should sweep and swab while boys repair the light bulbs or do the shopping are stereotypes to be junked along with the Suffering Sita role.

Successful women have asked their organizations for assistance and pushed the ecosystem around them to cater to the special needs that they have. If you are pulling your weight at work, and you believe you are an asset to your business and your boss, you should push for more women-friendly policies in case your organization doesn't have any. Lata asked us to create a crèche for her when she had a baby since she didn't have any help at home. She could then manage to continue working by bringing her baby and nanny to work with her every day. It benefited her as well as us, since not only did we manage to retain a high-performing employee but also the crèche ensured that we attracted more women to join us.

Many working women also create networks of support amongst their friends. So, apart from carpools and potlucks, I know women who make sure they have befriended parents with children in the same class so that they are kept abreast of the latest school news, projects, best tuitions to go to, etc. I realized how woefully inadequate I had been in that respect when once Sid's school picnic got cancelled late in the night and the only way parents got to know about it was through their own network. I was the only parent who landed up at 5 a.m. the next day, with Sid in tow, out of a class of ninety—everyone else was wired up to someone or the other. Don't make the same mistake I made!

CORPORATE MANTRA OF THE DAY

- To succeed, women need to create support systems around themselves at home and at work, by asking for help. Especially in the upbringing of children, it is important to have as much family help as possible—it really is true that 'It takes a village to bring up a child'.

- The reason why women hesitate to ask for help is that they fear the loss of control it will entail over some important portion of their life.

PSST...

- Ask your mother or mother-in-law for help in bringing up your baby. After all, they didn't do too bad a job in rearing you or your husband, did they?

- If you are a great worker, your organization will certainly try and create a supportive environment to help you manage the balance. (But if you are not, don't expect them to go out of their way.)

15

TAKING ADVANTAGE OF PRIVILEGES

DEALING WITH BENEFITS RESPONSIBLY

When we pressurize our organizations to create women-friendly policies for us (and, indeed, we must—not only for ourselves but so that the women who come into corporate life subsequently can also benefit), we need to understand the responsibility that comes along with these privileges. It is up to us to ensure that we do not take undue advantage of the flexibility we have got, and to prove to our organizations that we are exemplary employees and as good as (if not better than) our colleagues who have worked the full day when we were working for only half of it.

Fortunately, I have mostly come across women who are extremely conscientious and deeply cognizant of the burden of delivering results that comes along with the special privileges they get. In fact, a colleague who is working from home these days was telling me how guilty she feels if she gets up to make lunch or do some household chore during the typical 'office hours'.

However, once in a while you do encounter the Beenas of the world.

Beena, a producer in our creative team, seemed to always be going through some personal crisis or another. It was as if bad luck had marked her out for special treatment. She had a highly susceptible constitution and thus invariably fell sick with every single ailment doing the rounds; she had several friends and relatives who constantly needed her personal intervention in a faraway city, to save them from some catastrophe or the other; and, to top it all, there were deaths in the family with alarming regularity.

Initially, all of us felt extremely sorry for her and wondered how someone could be so ill-fortuned—until a grandmother passed away for the third time. Finally cottoning on to the fact that her ill luck was more a figment of her imagination than based in substance, we had to politely tell her to go. It was suggested to her that maybe the time had come to hand over charge to a person who could devote more hours to work, and that maybe she personally would benefit if she took up full-time employment in the service of her relatives and friends—it would pain us deeply to carry on without her in the organization, but we were ready and willing to make the attempt.

Another woman employee, who was ostensibly on a longish sick leave, posted pictures of herself holidaying abroad on Facebook. Obviously, she is now an ex-employee.

However, in nine cases out of ten, wherever women have got special privileges like flexi-timing, I have seen them work far more responsibly and with extra effort during the time they are in office.

But the elephant in the room that organizations today grapple with is not so much whether women are taking unwonted advantage but whether the fact that we are bending over backwards to be fair to women brings into play a sort of reverse bias. Are we then ending up being unfair to the men around us, who are getting the shorter end of the stick?

Consider the following scenario.

Assume there are two sales heads in an organization, one male and the other female. Both are equally competent and consequently always end up meeting their targets and achieving their objectives. They are at the same level and get the same incentive. Now, one year, the female sales head goes on maternity leave and takes the requisite three-month break, which by law and policy she is entitled to. In the nine months she has been working, she achieves her targets. Thus, when the time comes for disbursing her incentive, will she get the full amount or three-fourths, given that she has worked only nine out of the twelve months?

Theoretically, the answer may be an easy one, but when HR heads have to take these calls on the ground and in practice, it is not as simple as it looks. As per policy and her entitlement, she should get her full dues (after all, maternity leave is supposed to be a fully paid benefit), and that is only fair. But if she gets her full incentive, what about the male sales head who worked the full year? He will also end up getting the same amount in spite of having worked three more months than her. Is that fair? But, then, the reality is that she has to necessarily take time off for the delivery, which he doesn't. The counter to that is that many men do want more time off to spend with their babies but are entitled to only three days of paternity break. What about fairness there?

And so the never-ending circle of questions and doubts goes on. What is right and what is not? How do we balance being fair to both our male and female employees?

These are some of the difficulties an organization has to

deal with on a practical basis as they embark on the journey of managing diversity and, at the same time, being impartial to all their employees. Given this very difficult balance that progressive organizations are trying to achieve, let us not make their job unnecessarily difficult by exploiting the liberties that have been accorded to us—or, more importantly, have been fought for by the generation of feminists that came before us.

A multinational organization of Scandinavian origin has a nine-month paid maternity plan. Ashu, a batch mate who heads their sales and marketing function, informed me recently that he had decided not to recruit women in his team any longer. This was tantamount to waving a red flag in front of my eyes; I immediately raised my cudgels on behalf of the sisterhood and started questioning him sharply about his opinion of women employees, deriding him for being a nasty little MCP.

'Arre, nahin, my dear Jhansi ki Rani!' he protested. 'But what do I do? Any woman who is planning to have a baby in the near future joins us knowing about the nine-month paid leave policy. I have had three women in the last few months becoming pregnant within a month of joining us. Now, in a department of twelve people, with three members on leave, how do I manage, tell me?' He looked glumly at me.

As a manager, I empathize with him completely. As a woman, I worry. If we behave so irresponsibly and exploit organizations like this, what will happen to the reputation of working women and to the generations of women who will come after us? Will the privileges be taken away from them? (Or, maybe, there will be no further need for diversity policies since no one will want to recruit women any longer.)

Corporate mantra of the day

- It is important to work with your organization and create a win-win for both you and them by ensuring that they have women-supportive policies in place.
- It is equally critical that we don't take undue advantage of the privileges awarded to us and deliver value back to our organization.

Psst...

- No organization likes being exploited. It will backfire either on the women who are misusing the policies or, worse, on the women who come in after them.
- If you have perchance called in with the excuse of a stomach ache and gone off to the hills with your friends, at least don't put it up on Facebook—remember, you had befriended your boss on it only last month.

16

HUSBANDS TRAINED HERE

CREATING A SUPPORTIVE SPOUSE

One of the absolutely critical steps in the journey of adapting in order to reach the final stage of achievement is getting your husband-training right. Without this crucial piece in place, I assure you, it will not matter how hard you work or how much you persevere or get your organization to support you. You will not be able to move very far ahead until you get your spouse well and truly trained to cope with your career and its demands.

Unfortunately, a readymade supportive spouse is neither natural-born nor can you pluck him off a tree. You have to spend years gently nurturing and guiding him till, one fine day, he emerges from his chrysalis and all your friends look at you in envy and say: 'How lucky you are! Sanjay is so good with Sid. And he cooks so divinely too. Don't tell me he made that shepherd's pie all by himself?' And while he takes the bow, inwardly you preen. After all, who got him up to scratch? You accept the compliment graciously, mentally patting yourself on the back for a job well done. Little do your friends know that this has nothing to do with luck but more to do with loads of hard work and persistence on your part.

While there are, of course, the very rare exceptions in the husband brigade, men who have grown up believing women to be equal partners and have even been known to rustle up a gourmet meal on their wives' birthdays, most husbands belong to the TLT ('Tauliya Lao' Type) fraternity. A large number of this TLT brigade, I am sorry to say, come from my part of the country—North India, especially Delhi. Brought up as they are, with slavish adoration from their beta-crazy moms, they think the world owes them a living and everyone around them exists only to do their bidding. Even worse are men from South India who have lived for generations in Delhi. Like converts to another religion, they are more devout, and uphold the tenets of TLT-ism even more fanatically than their North Indian brethren.

A neighbour of ours is a senior income tax official from Ludhiana, and a king amongst the TLT clan. A typical morning in his life plays out like this.

'Aijee, your tea is ready.' His wife will try to wake him up, only to be greeted by a snore and a bit of mumbling from the TLT king as he lies dreaming of the next raid he is going to conduct at that hot actress's house. 'It will get cold, do get up.' Pushpa will nudge him again when he still hasn't got up ten minutes later.

This interplay is happening at about 9 a.m., when the rest of the neighbourhood has left a long while ago to catch their 7.57 a.m. locals and 8.05 a.m. ladies' specials. You can now probably appreciate why there is a long list of applicants for all the IT officials' entrance exams. Apart from the perks that come with either conducting or not conducting raids on diamond merchants, as the case may be, there is also the added advantage of reaching office at 11 a.m. and departing at 5 p.m. to go drinking at the IT club or whatever the appropriate watering hole for all hardworking income tax officials is. (Possibly a club whose owner has mysteriously escaped being raided for the past six months.)

Anyway, my neighbourhood TLT king finally gets up and, bleary-eyed, flops down at the dining table where the cup of tea and a neatly ironed newspaper are lying in pristine condition. Everyone in the family knows that no one should touch the paper before he reads it, lest it get crumpled. 'Ugh, the tea is cold!' He spits out the first mouthful. 'Pushpa, how many times have I told you that I hate cold tea?'

Instead of pouring it over his head and yelling that it's his bloody fault the tea has gone cold, which is what you and I would have done, Pushpa (not having read this book) apologizes profusely and scurries to the kitchen to get him another cup.

A hearty breakfast and an hour later, the TLT king prepares to leave for work. 'Pushpa, where is my towel?' He shouts from the bathroom. (Imagine the bathroom floor all wet and slippery as he waits for his towel, which he has forgotten to take for the nth time.) 'Pushpa, my shirt sleeves are not ironed properly.' 'Pushpa, my shoe polish.' 'Pushpa, my handkerchief.' 'Where, for God's sake, are the car keys? Why do you keep them away every day?'

'Hullo? *You* threw them on the sofa yesterday, what was I supposed to do?' Pushpa should ideally be saying. Instead, she scampers to and fro, dealing with all his kingly needs.

A carelessly thrown out 'Oh, by the way, a few of my friends are dropping in this evening to watch the match, just rustle up something, will you?', and off he goes with the wind to do important things in the office.

From past experience, Pushpa knows that 'a few' could mean anything from two to ten friends, and 'rustle up something' means a four-course meal at the very least. She calls to cancel her parlour appointment for the fifth time this month; after all, cleaning up after the TLT king and cooking dinner will take up the rest of the day, not to forget the children, their homework and their meals.

This, alas, is the raw material you have to start with when you begin the arduous task of husband-training, so you can understand how daunting your mission is. But don't get disheartened. If you persevere (and read on and follow a few of my suggestions), all your hard work will most certainly pay off.

When you start your husband-training routine, one of the things you have to realize is that men are strange creatures. Over the years, I have figured out that if you tell them something directly to their face they are more likely to bolt and run in the opposite direction. You have to nudge and hint and whisper and tell them stuff only when they are watching Sachin Tendulkar bat. And never ever look them directly in the face and give them orders—oops, I mean suggestions. Advice to men always has to be smuggled in, surreptitiously, while they are involved in doing other important things.

'I was thinking that if you could take Mummy to the doctor tomorrow, I can catch up with all the pending paperwork,' you suggest while vigorously dusting him and the couch he is sitting on and watching the match.

'Uh, what? Uff, move out of the way, you are standing right in front of the TV. Okay, I'll take her… OH, MY GOD, what a shot!'

You get the drift?

Yet another thing you have to keep in mind while training husbands is to take one particular aspect at a time, since the poor dears can't multitask anyway, and break them in gently, with a light but firm hand.

For example, I started the training process by inculcating in HD the fine art of listening. In the early days of our marriage, around the third sentence of me telling him about my day at work, he would get distracted by the song playing on the radio or the headlines of the paper (which he had already read) or a lateral thought in his mind. And I had to barely mention a problem at work to be given reams of advice. It has taken several years of implementing a rigorous training schedule involving the silent treatment, the indirect hints and the moist eyes. But I am proud to say that he has passed the Art of Listening course with flying colours by figuring out the following:

1. When I am talking to him, he needs to interject with many empathetic 'hmms' and 'oohs' and a few 'you poor things' at appropriate intervals. That's enough to hold up his end of the conversation, nothing more is required.
2. Giving advice is a big no-no. I don't tell him about the latest crisis at work so that I can take his advice. I already know what to do; I am just sharing my problems to bond with him better.

In fact, he has become so good now that he can listen to an entire litany of my predicaments while watching Sachin bat, without missing a single 'poor you' cue.

Once you have the hang of it, you can graduate to more complex training projects. Like how to manage the house when you are away on business trips without immediately calling out for help from his (or your) mother. Or how to fit in the PTA meetings with the office and golf schedule. Or even how to share equally in the task of child rearing.

When Sid's board exams were at hand, both HD and I decided to each take fifteen days off to help him with his last-minute revisions, etc. The first fifteen-day slot was mine, and

I diligently sat with the poor child from 10 a.m. to 10 p.m. as he swotted his way through reams of history, geography and EVED.

Then came HD's turn. Having had past experience of his operating style, I decided that I would overlap one day with him in order to ensure that everything went as per expectations. I had vaguely overheard him talk to his brother and holiday, beer and golf were some of the words that were being bandied around a bit too freely for my liking. Naturally, I was a little concerned.

Sure enough, HD got up early in the morning and, after giving Sid breakfast and hustling him to get ready, deposited him with his books at the study table. His next steps of preparation involved putting several bottles of beer in the fridge, dragging his rocking chair in front of the TV and avidly scrutinizing the TV schedule in the papers for details of the next match.

'What exactly are you planning to do today?' I asked him sweetly.

'Why? Supervise Sid's studies, of course.' He looked at me wide-eyed. 'You don't worry, go to office, you have already taken two weeks off. Now carry on, you'll get late.' He patted me heartily on my back, pushing me towards the door.

'And how do you plan to keep an eye on him while you are sitting here in the bedroom, watching a match?' I glared at him.

'Oh, very simple. Like this... SID, ARE YOU STUDYING?' he roared from the bedroom.

'Yes, Papa!' Sid sang back from the study table in his room, playing book cricket with his scale and eraser.

'See, I'll keep checking like this once in a while. Chill, my dear, I have everything under control.' He gave me a reassuring smile.

This was one of the occasions when I decided mild remonstration would not work. So I launched into HD, recounting in excruciating detail how I had sat with Sid for hours at a stretch to ensure he focused on his study material, getting up from the table only to get his meals on time. And how sitting and watching a match in the next room at deafening levels was not exactly suited to creating a conducive atmosphere at home for serious studies, given the sports-mad genes Sid has inherited from his father.

The shock treatment paid off and all went well for the balance fourteen days of supervision by HD.

While I explicitly recommend kindness and gentle nudging as a training method, once in a while it's worth trying the tough cop routine. That delivers results too.

CORPORATE MANTRA OF THE DAY

- A supportive spouse is a fundamental necessity if women want to make a success of their professional and personal lives.
- Unfortunately, readymade helpful husbands are in short supply, so they need to be trained according to our requirements.

PSST...

- Husband-training is a slow and fine art which needs to be perfected over decades of living together. Don't assume you will get there in the first few years of married life.
- Follow the 'water dripping on a stone' approach. Gentle nagging works better than yelling, which should be used only once in a while as shock treatment!

17

BEING THE BOSS IS RELATIVE

YOU DON'T HAVE TO BE ON TOP ALL THE TIME

HD strides into the house purposefully. 'APU, WHERE ARE YOU?' he calls out in a stentorian tone. The fact that I have opened the door for him seems to have escaped his attention. 'Did you ask the vet to come and check Scamper?' Scamper is our one-eyed cocker spaniel and a valued member of the household for the last eleven years. 'And his medicines? Did you send Sakharam to get them?' Sakharam is our driver, equally valued, fortunately two-eyed. 'And didn't you speak to the fruitwallah?' HD's special friend, who has been supplying horrendously expensive fruit to us for the last eight years and, in the process, has built a pucca house for himself and his five brothers. 'He called up wanting to know when he should do his delivery. Didn't I ask you to tell him to come today?'

My head starts spinning with a feeling of deja vu. I think these are the exact instructions I had given HD the previous night, albeit in far more dulcet tones—so why is he playing them back to me?

The next moment, Sid walks in. 'Mummy, I thought you were supposed to call the vet? I told you yesterday...' He gives me an accusing look, bending down to pet Scamper, who's looking just as accusingly at me, obviously feeling betrayed by my failure at not taking his health seriously.

The problem in our household is that all members think they are the CEO. So everyone goes around ordering everyone else to do the work, doing nothing themselves. The Purohit family, therefore, is very high on strategy but fares quite poorly in execution. Like all MDs, we keep giving instructions, expecting everyone else to fall in line, little realizing that the other person is doing exactly the same.

To be fair, you can't blame us completely. We are a classic example of 'Some people being born to CEO-ship (Sid), some people achieving CEO-ship (Sanjay) and some people having CEO-ship thrust upon them (me).' So, while Sid thinks he was born to lead and not follow, HD has been very clear from his management trainee days that he would start running organizations as soon as he could, and I got thrust, somewhat precipitously and unknowingly, into running departments and organizations at a very early age.

Apart from summarily giving commands to all and sundry, we also have a distinct aversion to taking orders from anyone, often under the mistaken belief that we know it all. (Aha! Does that remind you of someone in the higher echelons of your organization perhaps?)

This particular dislike became startlingly evident when we were on a self-driven holiday in Tuscany recently. Typically on such holidays, I am the official navigator, poring over the AAA map, planning out the itinerary, deciding which sights to see, whether we would whizz across the highway or take the scenic route, and so on. This time, however, the family decided that the time had come to graduate to the digital world and thus we should invest in a GPS.

So Tim-the-GPS was duly installed and we set off on our travels. The first journey with Tim giving us instructions in his quiet, imposing voice and polished upper-class accent went well. We reached the little village in Tuscany that was to be our home for the next ten days without much ado. However, little did we know that Sanjay-the-husband had taken a deep and violent dislike to Tim-the-GPS. Maybe it was that authoritative tone, which reminded him of a school principal, or maybe it was the inherent aversion we all have to taking orders, or maybe it was just one more example of men not asking for directions.

The next day, we realized, much to our consternation, that every time Tim would say something HD would want to do exactly the opposite since, according to him, Tim was a fool and an idiot. And every time it would require gentle cajoling from me and Sid before he would agree to follow what Tim was saying. Since this invariably happened at crossroads and roundabouts where decisions need to be taken in split seconds, it created a lot of stress and drama in the car. But we more or less ended up reaching where we had intended to go in the first place.

And then Tim let us down very badly and dropped us like a ton of bricks in the middle of nowhere. While looking for a highly recommended restaurant in a small town near the Tuscan coast, Tim took us on a wild goose chase that involved going up and down a steep road three times, turning two loops back on the route we had originally taken and finally stopping in the middle of a forest with not a soul in sight, where in a self-satisfied tone Tim announced, 'You have reached your destination.'

This, of course, immediately confirmed to HD that he had been right all along in branding Tim an idiot. No explanations from us—that we had possibly typed in the wrong address, or that finding a small restaurant is not really a GPS's core competency—would make him change his opinion.

We finally did not find the restaurant, ate at the nearest place we could get to and decided to drive back home. But HD had decided that, in the Sanjay vs Tim stand-off, this episode had tilted the scales in his favour. At the very next roundabout, with a manic and determined glint in his eye, he swung the car in exactly the direction away from Tim's recommendation.

We watched in horrified silence as with every passing mile away from the correct route Tim's voice kept mounting in hysteria and he went into paroxysms of panic. Every time Tim would ask us to turn back, HD would press the accelerator even harder. By the time we had driven fifty-odd miles, poor Tim had hyperventilated himself into oblivion, and all of us had realized that we were completely lost.

Thankfully, the signposts on the Italian highways are clear and we reached home finally, though not without adding 100 extra miles and several tiring hours to our journey.

You can see what a headstrong family we are!

In spite of that, though, I think we have managed to chug along quite well with each other. Give or take a few slanging matches and a couple of fistfights (I joke!), life has been fairly peaceful, and I honestly believe it has a lot to do with both HD and me being willing to be adaptable and wearing a different hat at home than we do at work.

So, while in office we operate in the command-and-control style of functioning and are very independent about the decisions we take, at home we both make an attempt to be more compliant and adjusting, even agreeably playing passive roles in certain situations. (Me in kitchen management, as you have figured out by now.) There is no point in both of us taking control of investments or holiday plans, for instance. One person takes the lead, and the other is happy to follow (throwing in unwanted advice once in a while just to demonstrate that we haven't given up every ounce of control, though).

Therein resides the secret of combining a happy marriage with a successful career, I think. As we become more senior at work, we start getting used to being in charge and taking the lead position in any situation. But marriage is an equal partnership that can't survive if both parties want to be the leader and in control every time and in every situation. It requires adaptability in roles, the ability to give and take and a willingness to relinquish charge. We must manage this partnership through consensus, not control.

CORPORATE MANTRA OF THE DAY

• Certain situations expect you to take charge and certain situations require you to give up control. Be willing to adapt and change according to the need.

PSST...

• You don't need to always be the boss at home too. Give up the responsibility of being in charge once in a while and enjoy playing the helpless woman.

18

THE SUM OF THE PARTS IS IMPORTANT

THINKING OF THE FAMILY AS A UNIT

'Vijay and I are getting divorced,' Smita announced, plopping into the chair next to mine at the restaurant where we were meeting for lunch.

'WHAT? When? How? Why?' Both the waiter, who was setting the table and paying close attention to the conversation, and I were completely taken aback at the sudden proclamation and gaped at Smita in shocked wonder, waiting with bated breath to be enlightened further.

Smita and I have been friends for the last twenty years, having graduated from college together and more or less remained in touch throughout. Both HD and I have known Vijay and her for almost the entire time they have been married and always considered them to be a happy, well-adjusted couple. They had no children, but both had very busy and fulfilling lives in the corporate world.

'Relax, yaar, don't stare at me like a fish.' Smita frowned at me. 'You, can you get us the menu please? I am sure you are eager to know how the rest of the story proceeds, but we are hungry!' she said sarcastically to the waiter. She turned back to me. 'Anyway, there is nothing to be concerned about. It is all very civilized. You know we haven't exactly been getting along too well...' No, I did not know! 'We've sort of drifted apart in the last few years, so we thought what's the point in being miserable with each other, better to enjoy ourselves independently. We are going tomorrow to sign the papers. It's called divorce by mutual consent.'

'So quickly? Smita, have you thought this through? Have you talked to a counsellor? Isn't it too drastic? Why don't you spend some time figuring out the issues... Can I help? Why didn't you tell me?' Dismayed, I tried to grapple with the magnitude of what she was telling me.

'Uff, don't be such a wimp. Both of us are very clear about the step we are taking—we are not impulsive teenagers. In fact, we are planning to have a party to celebrate our divorce. It's next Saturday—obviously, you are invited—and the theme is Freedom,' she declared grandiloquently. 'You should have seen the expression on the lawyer's face when we were working out our divorce settlement. He couldn't believe it was happening in such an amicable fashion. We sorted out all the property and other issues in one hour flat,' Smita nattered on.

'But how do you go about doing this kind of a thing? You must have quite a lot of stuff that you jointly purchased over the years? Coupled with the trauma of the divorce, to also go through the process of deciding how to share...' My voice trailed off as I cast my mind to all the art and jewellery and properties Vijay and Smita had been buying over the years.

Having reassured myself that Smita wasn't exactly sounding heartbroken, I had moved on to the more practical aspects

of the separation. My curiosity was aroused and I wanted
to understand the nuances of separating after twenty years
of living together. (After all, it's always good to know how
such things are done—you never know when the information
might come in handy. When HD hassles me, I often fantasize
about running away...now I could have more fun imagining
what goodies I would run away with!)

'Oh, very simple,' Smita said, digging into her pasta while
the waiter (he of the inquisitive ear) set everything on the
table as slowly as possible so that he had a front row seat to
the dramatic narration for as long as he could manage. 'We
just divided things according to who had bought them... So
the Gurgaon house is mine and the land in Noida is his. The
refrigerator is mine and the two TV sets he bought go to him.
Only, you remember the Krishna painting that you also liked
very much? It was my favourite, but he had bought it with
his money. I remember I hadn't carried my cheque book that
day. So that's gone to him!' She sighed as she took a long sip
of her mojito.

'Hullo?' I was totally perplexed. 'What do you mean his
money and yours?' Having always maintained joint accounts
with HD, which presumably all married couples do, I didn't
quite understand this notion of mine and yours. Our house
(and everything else in it) is in both HD's and my names, and
I don't even remember which account the refrigerator was
bought from (not that it matters, since they are in any case
joint accounts).

'Well, we have been very clear from day one about
maintaining separate accounts and keeping everything we
own separate, in our individual names. Don't tell me you
haven't done the same? Oh, my dear, how middle class of
you!' Smita chortled. 'And with you earning a fat salary all
this while and giving all these speeches about emancipation...

Haha!' She doubled up with mirth, the quickly quaffed mojito adding an extra cackle to her laughter.

Speechless, I experienced some uneasy qualms. Was I really not as independent as I thought? Had HD been surreptitiously running my life all these years just because we had joint accounts?

Fortunately, better sense prevailed and I quickly got back to my usual practical self. It seemed to me that by keeping everything separate and marking the fixed assets register with 'yours' and 'mine' tags, Vijay and Smita had been preparing for divorce almost from the day they got married. In my humble opinion, half the root cause of all marital strife is when each person thinks of themselves only as an individual entity in the relationship and misses the point that they are now part of a family unit.

Maintaining one's individuality within a marriage is obviously important and essential, but working together to ensure the success of the entire family is paramount too. And, as in all teams, the larger interest of the team has to start outweighing the needs of the singular player at some point.

So, is it individual need or greater good? This issue raises its head and creates conflict several times in our married lives, but I have often seen it come up specifically when both spouses are working and one partner wants to move to another city or country in the interest of their career. What should the other spouse do, especially if their career is going well? Give up their job? Stay separately?

Various families have tried different solutions and, indeed, it is a very tough choice with no easy answers. At that point, the only thing one can do is to ask what is in the benefit of the family as a whole. Sometimes the answer requires one partner to compromise, and sometimes the other partner has to give up that lucrative offer. As long as both parties recognize that it can never be only the woman adjusting all the time and that a situation may arise when the husband too has to take a backseat for the family's good, all is well.

The happy news is that, many a time when we think we are taking the sidetrack so that our better halves can run on the main course, the by-lanes can actually throw up some interesting possibilities. Life can be quite tricky, in that sense.

Sujata had to take some time off when her husband got transferred to Netherlands on a two-year project, but she used those two years effectively and got certified in an international tax programme and, as a consequence, when they came back to India she got a fantastic position with a global conglomerate.

When HD had to move to Chennai, I left my job with the advertising agency I loved with a heavy heart. But in the new organization I joined, I ended up interacting with the president of the company on several new business initiatives. The aforesaid gentleman was subsequently responsible for the big break I got in my career five years later.

So, you just never know what twists and turns are in store for you. Therefore, at every juncture where you have to take the tough decision, just go with the one that is in the best interest of the family. I promise you will never regret it.

CORPORATE MANTRA OF THE DAY

- It is important to think of the family as a team, a composite whole rather than a collection of individual, discrete parts. Any sports manager will tell you that no team succeeds if each player thinks only of himself.
- When there comes a time in your life where a decision

has to be made which requires compromise, go for the one which maximizes the family's interest.

PSST...

- If you have somewhere taken a backseat with the family's genuine interest at heart, things will turn out in your favour. Trust your karma on that.
- Don't forget to work hard during that phase too. Someone is always watching. But more of that in Chapter 29.

19

MASTERING NETWORKING

GROUP THERAPY

As part of my job, I have to travel to Mumbai from Bangalore frequently. As you may know, the journey to the Bangalore airport is quite a long one. (Many people maintain that, owing to an error, the Bangalore airport has been built in Hyderabad whilst the Hyderabad airport has been built in Bangalore.) As it happens, this journey gives all of us frequent travellers loads of time to do some deep thinking and introspection, especially early in the morning.

On one such trip, I was chatting with Swami, the driver, and suddenly realized that I always ended up tipping him double of what I gave the other drivers. The transport vendor our company uses has a roster of drivers who come to pick me, and they are all very decent. And it isn't that Swami is a better driver, or more prompt, or the car in better shape; all the drivers I have interacted with provide equally good service.

When I analysed this, I figured out that the only difference between Swami and the other drivers is that he has managed to build a relationship with me. Unlike the other drivers who only focus on the job, which is driving me to and from the airport, Swami invests in wanting to know more about me, in what I do, where and why I travel so much. Part of this is because he is an incorrigible talker, but partly it is also because he is interested in me as an individual.

So, our early-morning conversations range from nostalgia about the 'olden-golden days' of Bangalore as he likes to call them ('When, madam, the air was so clean that you only inhaled pure oxygen and you never ever needed to use a fan throughout the year') to politics and politicians, on which he has very spurious but decided opinions ('That CM! Madam, she is very evil, let me tell you. As soon as she comes to power, she starts asking for water from Karnataka. That's because she is a Brahmin you see! Brahmins have this big greed for water, madam. For centuries they have been hoarding water and troubling the poor...'). Swami also regales me with entertaining but unbelievable anecdotes about some of his clients, including a bizarre one about a female client in the Middle East who needed to be taken to the ICU practically daily because she used to choke on her food—according to Swami, her windpipe and food pipe had got intertwined(!) and he took her to hospital no less than 150 times in his tenure there. Equally implausible are the stories about religion which he loves to narrate. Although a Christian, he has a pantheonic belief in all gods, as evidenced by the range of holy images decorating his dashboard and his numerous visits to various temples and churches of South India. 'My wife had the shivering disease, madam, and her hands and feet had curled up so much that she used to just lie in bed all day and had not walked for a month till I took her to Velankanni. And then, madam, a miracle happened. I lifted her from the car and took her inside the church and she immediately started walking!'

Swami also worries about me. 'You travel so much, madam. Do you eat your meals on time? Drink lots of cow's milk, it is better than buffalo milk. But donkey's milk is the best, we used to drink it in the olden-golden days...' And so on.

Coming back to the point: I realized that I was paying a premium not for the service (which was outstanding across drivers) but for the bond Swami had managed to build with me. The reality is that all of us value relationships and, knowingly or unknowingly, want connections with neighbours, colleagues and even fellow travellers.

Women, I think, are especially good at this. From the time of having been left behind in caves while our men went hunting, we have lived and worked in groups and communal environments. Thus we have a natural affinity towards building networks of support. However, paradoxically, I see that many times women fail at building professional networks for themselves. Especially when they get married and have children—because they are trying to balance family and work, they lose out on this important part of their lives.

In fact, many women themselves have acknowledged their failure to do so and often quote not having professional networks as one of the top three reasons for not moving ahead in their careers.

So, if women are genetically and naturally inclined towards building clusters, and if they understand that it is detrimental to their careers to not do so, why don't they go ahead and do something about it?

'What a question! Where is the time?' huffs Priya. 'I run from office as soon as I can so that I can be home in time to help Akshay with his studies, then organize the meals, the next day's dabbas... And weekends? Hah. Weekends are for chores and more chores.'

'And we don't drink or smoke, so those interminable after-office sessions at the club that boss has, we don't enjoy going there. Inevitably, only the boys in the team go with him,' adds Sheila. 'But it's true that having some sort of equation beyond work helps. I realized that when I couldn't call up my old boss for some help I wanted with my new job since I didn't know him at all beyond work,' she says.

'I agree. My husband has his squash-playing group of buddies at the gym, then his school friends and his IIT alumni association, so when he was looking for additional assignments for his legal practice, he got at least half of them from that lot itself,' pipes up Anuja.

Half the reason for not having these networks in place is the fact that the corporate environment is geared towards handling the lifestyles of employees who have support (read 'wife') at home. So men can spend that extra time beyond work investing in networking, knowing that there is someone at home to keep that front going, while women cannot. Indeed, I often joke that all professional women require a wife at home!

The other reason is that up until now there was not enough critical mass for women to network, even if they made the time. Typically, your boss and your super-boss were male, as were 90% of your colleagues. Their networking tended to revolve around manly things like the bar or the golf course, which didn't appeal to most women. It is only now, as more and more women get into middle and senior roles, that there are enough of them to create their own networking forums.

So my advice to you is: don't give up on this important tool of getting ahead in the race. Do make the effort to build a professional network, interact with more women in your domain and attend more industry events. If nothing else, at least start your very own version of a corporate kitty party. It can be of tremendous help, I assure you.

CORPORATE MANTRA OF THE DAY

- A lack of networking at the professional level is being considered as one of the critical factors by women themselves in their failure to move ahead in the corporate race.
- Building relationships beyond work with employees, colleagues and clients is a very important part of success.

PSST...

- If you sincerely want to help women do better in the corporate world, why don't you start your own mentoring or networking forum geared specifically towards women?

20

ARE YOU THE VICTIM OR THE HEROINE OF YOUR STORY?

MAKING LEMONADE OUT OF THE LEMONS THROWN AT YOU

The last and final lesson in adapting your way towards achievement is to understand that no one except you is responsible for the role you want to play in the drama of your life. So, whether you are going to be the heroine of your story or the victim or even a disinterested onlooker as life passes by, the choice is completely yours to make—not your husband's, mother-in-law's or boss's.

Viji is a classic example of someone who took control of her own life and demonstrated to everyone that each of us can attain whatever we want, provided we have the determination to catch life by its horns and ride the tiger. (I am mixing metaphors here, and tigers don't have horns, but you get what I mean.)

Viji got married at the age of eighteen. By the time she turned twenty-two, she was already the mother of two daughters. In the four years that had passed, she had also realized that her husband was a bit of a wastrel. He had big dreams but little capability to make a success of them. So, in quick succession, he had tried running an agency for a gas company, worked for a few months in a BPO and tried (unsuccessfully) to get a job in the Middle East. The only result of all these endeavours was the quick erosion of the dowry that Viji had brought with her, along with the limited savings the couple had. The husband finally decided that the problem was Chennai, where they resided, and so they shifted, bag and baggage, to Bangalore, where according to him they were destined to make their fortune.

'I later figured out that he actually moved to Bangalore to escape the recriminations of his relatives for not being able to take care of his family, as well as the loans he had surreptitiously taken from them,' said Viji wryly as she narrated her story to a group of us at the Women Entrepreneurs Forum. 'Anyway, I had two mouths to feed, so I started giving Bharatnatyam classes in my neighbourhood to pay for the rent and household expenses. In the meantime, he and his friend went and applied to become distributors of a big power generating company that was starting operations in South India. I don't know how, but they managed to get the distributorship for one part of Bangalore. It started with much fanfare, but within a year he had, as usual, lost interest and was ready to give that up too.

'By this time, I had figured out that the tuition fees I was earning was barely helping make ends meet and I needed to do something more. So I told him that I would run the distributorship. Everyone laughed at me. "You can't even speak English. And do you even understand what a generator looks like?" they taunted.

'But I was determined. I went to the regional head of the

company and asked him to let me run it and not take back the distributorship. He too laughed at me. "Running a business is not like running your kitchen, my dear. Do you know what is debit and credit?" he asked me. I offered him a deal: if I didn't get any orders within the next three months, he could take the distributorship back. By God's grace, he was busy with expansion plans in the rest of the South markets and didn't have the time to look for an alternate distributor, so he agreed to give me three more months.

'I then went across to my neighbour, a kind man, who owned a business and asked him for help. He sat me down and explained the nitty-gritties of the job, including helping me create invoices on the computer. I visited every small business in my area in the first month and, fortunately, got a couple of orders in the second month. After that, there was no looking back. Today, I am the largest distributor for the company in South India. I employ forty people and have bought the entire three floors of the house in which we had rented two small rooms. One of my daughters is an engineer and the other is an accomplished Bharatnatyam dancer. God has been kind...' Viji ended her story with tears in her eyes.

Time and again, I have seen that successful women don't necessarily start off with additional benefits. But, like Viji, they actually become successful by ensuring that whatever situations they face, adverse or otherwise, they are able to overcome and convert them to their advantage.

All of us were bowled over by Viji's courage and determination. Her story is inspirational to many women who struggle with similar issues of having to become breadwinners without the support of an education or an enabling family background. It is an eye-opener for all of us who have not faced the kind of travails she has had to contend with. Hats off to her, and may her tribe continue to grow!

CORPORATE MANTRA OF THE DAY

- Only you have control over your destiny. You can choose which role you want to play in your story.
- The difference between women who are successful and happy and those who are not is not in their special circumstances but in their ability to overcome every circumstance and make it special.

PSST...

- Sometimes, we deliberately choose to play victims. (Remember Suffering Sita?) Don't do that; otherwise, before you know it, it will become a mindset and a force of habit.

THE TEN LESSONS OF ADAPTING

1. **I will approach life with a positive mindset**

   When I strive towards achieving success, I realize that having a positive attitude is the first step. I will win the battle in my mind first.

2. **I will always work hard**

   I realize that running away from hard work is running away from success. The single most important driver of success in life is perseverance, and women who have triumphed have done so only because they simply didn't give up.

3. **I will learn to focus on the essential things and sacrifice the unimportant**

   Being able to prioritize what is important and what is not is a key skill for success. We don't need to be perfect; it is better to be outstandingly great at the specific areas we have chosen to focus on.

4. **I will ask for help in order to have a successful career and home life**

   We need to create support systems around ourselves at home and at work, by asking for help, and we should not worry about the loss of control it may entail.

5. **I will not take advantage of the special privileges I get for being a woman**

   It is critical that we don't take undue advantage of the privileges awarded to us and deliver value back to our organizations. We need to behave with responsibility, especially in the interests of the future generations of women who will come after us.

6. **I will have to train my husband to be a part of my support system**

   A supportive spouse is a fundamental requirement if we want to make a success of our professional and personal lives. Unfortunately, readymade helpful husbands are in short supply and need to be trained.

7. **I do not need to be the boss in every situation**

   Certain situations expect us to take charge and certain situations require us to give up control. We need to adapt and change according to the circumstances.

8. **I will be a team player in my family**

   It is important to think of the family as a composite whole and, therefore, when there comes a time in our life where a decision has to be made which requires compromise, it is crucial to go for the one which maximizes the entire family's interest.

9. **I will build relationships beyond work and use the power of networking**

   A lack of networking at the professional level is being seen as one of the critical factors by women themselves in their failure to move ahead in the corporate race. It is important that we make time to build these formal or informal networks.

10. **I will take control of my own destiny**

   The difference between women who are successful and happy and those who are not is not in their special circumstances but in their ability to take control of any circumstance and make it special.

PART III

ACHIEVEMENT

The final stage. A sense of accomplishment—hard won, but oh so sweet!

21

OYE, LUCKY MADAM!

APPRECIATING OUR GOOD FORTUNE

We have now reached the third and concluding lap of our journey together, you and I. And I hope you have been with me every step of the way, as together we first figured out how to bite the bullet and accept some basic realities, both pleasant and unpleasant, of being a working woman. At the second stage, we learnt to intelligently adapt our circumstances to suit us and make our situation work in favour of us. And, now, we are at the summit of our endeavours.

These last few steps will show us that when we achieve success there are certain patterns of behaviour we need to adopt. So that we can confidently wear the badge of our accomplishments and fly our banner high—whether it is in standing up for ourselves, or not running away from achievement, or learning to take pride in whatever we have done without being affected by negative people, or not allowing our own mindset to diminish our triumphs.

We women actually have very simple needs indeed. Give or take a few diamonds, about forty pairs of shoes, a few cuddles from our spouses and a reliable cook, all we want is to be happy and successful—both in our corporate lives and at home. We want to have a satisfying profession which helps us maximize our potential and a contented home life, with neither of the two obstructing each other.

Fortunately, in today's day and age, it is certainly possible to do this. Especially for a girl who has been born into a normal middle-class family in any urban city in the democratic world, the advantages of an education, of using that education to get a job and of becoming financially independent are all there for her to grab.

We are blessed to have lived in this era and in this environment, where no one questions whether their daughters should go to school or not, or whether the young lady who has graduated from college should work or not. Everywhere you look around, in a metro city in India today, parents are pushing their daughters to study and to work. She may be the daughter of a professor or a bank manager or a driver or even the peon in your office, but most parents are willing to give the same opportunities to their daughter as they have been giving to their sons.

Obviously, this is not the situation in many countries across the globe, nor is it the same in the villages of India. Neither was it the case with most women of our mothers' generation. Even today, the percentage of working women in India is a dismal 5-10% within the organized sector. Therefore, all of us who have both the ability and the freedom to work should count ourselves truly fortunate.

Yet we let go of this opportunity so easily sometimes.

'Ma'am, I am getting married, see my engagement ring.' The blushing bride-to-be, Neha, steps forward eagerly to show me the rock on her finger. I am visiting our Ahmedabad station and spending time with the team there during the annual review, along with the HR head.

'Congratulations, my dear! And what does your fiancé do?'

'Oh, he runs a business, ma'am. In fact, he is the grandson of...' And she names one of the big business families of the city.

The HR head and I look at each other. The first thought that is coursing through both our minds is: will Neha quit her job now? And regrettably but typically, that is the first reaction we have when we hear about someone getting engaged or married or becoming pregnant in our office. 'Will she leave now? Shit, I will have to start searching for a replacement again. And just as our attrition rates were dropping! Oh, why did I recruit a woman?'

Yes, ironically, in spite of being diversity conscious and women ourselves, as managers we struggle with this very challenge because many a time recruiting women comes with the added baggage of having to manoeuvre corporate requirements around their specific issues.

'So, what is your plan after marriage, Neha?' asks the HR head.

'I don't know, but I don't think he wants me to work...' Neha says coyly.

'And are you planning to always do what he tells you to?' comments the HR head wryly.

'You are teasing me, ma'am.' Neha pouts. 'My in-laws feel that there is no need for me to work, given their family background.' She sounds awed.

And, just like that, Neha is ready to walk away from all the hard work she has put in to get that management degree, the extraordinary hours of effort to achieve her sales targets, the rewards and recognition she has got for being a star performer in Ahmedabad station—simply because she is getting married.

Sadly, we see this story play out time and again, especially since we have a high ratio of women in our organization. We know that, sooner or later, maybe in a couple of years or maybe after fifteen years, when the children have grown up and flown the nest, Neha will regret this decision; but we also know that no amount of convincing from us will make a difference right now.

I want to shake Neha hard and point out the innumerable examples of women who haven't had the opportunities she is throwing away so lightly. The young student in a deeply conservative region of the world who gets shot because she wants to study. The society lady who has diamonds and rubies and designer clothes aplenty but has never signed a cheque in her life because she has no account of her own; every time she wants something, she has to go to her husband who can choose to give or not give her pin money, depending on his mood. I want to tell Neha about the women in the village nearby who have for the first time in their lives felt self-esteem and pride because an NGO is training them as anganwadi teachers and they can finally earn some money of their own; even their own families are treating them with far more respect than they had got before—after all, they are now bringing in some moolah, aren't they?

But I know it will make no difference. Neha is in the starry-eyed phase of her life and she doesn't want anyone to spray her rose-tinted glasses with a dose of reality and interfere with her romantic notions.

As we celebrate our success and our achievement, we must count ourselves blessed for being in the situation we are in today. Life has given us countless opportunities that millions of women don't have and will not get, at least in this lifetime. We must think a thousand times before we throw them away so lightly and carelessly! Marriage, a fight with a colleague, a tough assignment, a rotten day at work—these are absolutely no reasons to walk away from our hard-won accomplishments, and yet we make that mistake again and again.

CORPORATE MANTRA OF THE DAY

- A majority of the women in the world don't get the opportunity of an education and a chance to earn that many of us today take for granted.
- Let us remember always how lucky we are to be born in an era and in a milieu that has allowed us this freedom, and let us be cognizant and appreciative of that opportunity.

PSST...

- We often delude ourselves into thinking that it's a temporary break we are taking. I assure you that, once you leave the race, many of you will never come back.
- While earning the love of your family is good, earning their respect is important too. Very often, that comes if you are an earning member of the family.

22

AVOIDING THE MR & MRS TRAP

MAINTAINING ONE'S INDIVIDUALITY

One of the pet grouses women have (but don't voice) is that, after marriage, their identities invariably get subsumed into those of their husbands. They are no longer individuals in their own right but the add-on part of a couple, almost like the supplementary credit card that has no standing of its own.

Having had a fairly distinct existence of my own by virtue of my career, I didn't figure out this angst till I shifted to Bangalore, away from Mumbai—which had hitherto defined my actuality and where everyone in my social circle was aware of what I did. In Bangalore, however, things turned out to be markedly different.

HD's new job had taken him there, and I moved to be with him, so inevitably the people we met were those whom he knew from work. And every time I encountered new people, the introductions would go something like this: 'Meet Sanjay, he is the MD of ABC and has recently moved to Bangalore; he was with XYZ earlier. And, umm, this is his wife...' People would smile and shake hands and ask intelligent questions about HD's new job and the conversation would flow around his work, both present and past. As the by-the-way appendage, if at all the conversation veered towards me, it was to check on children, schooling and how I was settling into Bangalore.

I was quite flabbergasted since we working women are used to being defined by our corporate personas rather than our homemaker ones—a persona that, in my case, is only partially developed. So, suddenly, when I was stripped of being seen as a working woman, I didn't quite know how to handle it. The guys would all go and stand next to the bar and discuss the economy and the state of business and when the PM would finally announce policy changes, while I would get caught up in a group which wanted to talk about shopping and schooling.

I would gaze longingly at the assembly around the bar, wanting to escape there, both to get a drink as well as to discuss my business. Unfortunately, every time I tried sauntering towards them, the men would stop talking business and start asking me stilted questions about how I was coping with Bangalore. It just didn't occur to them that possibly I too was a working woman and that they could talk shop with me.

The incident that finally drove me up the wall was a peculiar conversation I had with our new neighbours. Our building in Bangalore is filled with expats from all over the world, or NRIs who have relocated temporarily to India on work. As is to be expected, the NRIs are more foreign than the expats and behave as if they have landed in some alien country rather than at the very place where they were eating curd rice with their fingers not so long ago.

'Hey, how'ya doing?' squealed my NRI neighbour when I got into the lift with her.

'Er, I am fine. And how are you?' I smiled politely.

'Getting along, getting along... Though, I must say, your systems here are a bit strange.' The twang in her voice got stronger.

Excuse me? *Our* systems? As far as I knew, she had been born and brought up in India and had moved to the US only a few years ago. I was ready to shoot off a sarcastic rejoinder when her husband joined us, energetically bounding into the lift, dressed to go jogging in a blinding yellow tracksuit.

'Hi, girls, gossiping already? Haha!' He looked at me and smirked. 'Prabha has been feeling quite lonely, but now that you have moved in, you girls must get together over coffee soon. I am sure you will become best of friends. And before we know it, you will be organizing kitty parties and shopping expeditions together, haha!'

I stared nastily at him and gritted my teeth in irritation. First of all, he had no business clubbing me in the 'you girls' category. (No one has called me a girl for twenty years, and I am just fine with that, thank you very much.) Secondly, I resented the fact that he had automatically assumed that I didn't work. Thirdly, even if I didn't work, I didn't see why he should assume that homemaker women only do two things: go for kitty parties and go shopping. I know several women who don't work in traditional jobs but still do several interesting things. (Including some women who have made gymming their career choice! When a friend of mine was introducing herself at a group therapy session and telling people about her job, that she was in sales, another lady responded with: 'Oh, how interesting, I do gymming.' But I digress.)

When I very firmly declined my neighbour's offer of getting together with his 'girl', saying that I was a working person and that, frankly, I didn't have the time, both of them were quite taken aback by my response.

'Oh, really? What do you do?' They looked puzzled, as if the concept of working women was foreign to them.

'I work with Radio City.'

'Are you an RJ?'

I don't know why people assume that if you work in a radio station you can only be an RJ. 'No, I run Radio City,' I retorted.

'Run?' They looked at me uncomprehendingly. 'Oh, you handle administration and travel and things like that. Nice...' They nodded and smiled beatifically, pleased that they had slotted me correctly.

Very often, I let people think whatever they want when I tell them I run the network—I find it very pompous to say that I am the CEO. But I was irritated beyond belief by now, so I looked at them firmly in the eye and said, 'Actually, I am the CEO.'

Now they were truly startled. 'Okay, very nice,' they murmured and sidled out of the lift.

These assumptions and this kind of typecasting happen all the time to a woman. Especially when a woman is married— she is immediately delegated to the shadow position. She is always the addendum and never the primary part of the couple. When she is single, people at least assume that since she is not married she must be doing something to keep herself busy and out of trouble, like working. That, of course, is yet another stereotyping saga (which we will discuss shortly).

I think the time has come to say that enough is enough and to get people to stop this pigeon-holing. The fact is that we, as women, have achieved a lot and now it is up to us to stand up and demand that we be counted in our own right—and we will assert ourselves loudly if required. If people keep making false assumptions, they need to be corrected, and corrected quickly; politeness needn't stand in the way.

Indeed, whenever any of our mutual acquaintances call me and ask me to follow up with HD on some invitation they have sent, or some request they have made, I very firmly tell them that I am not his secretary and they would be better advised to check with his office directly. And I have made it a habit to always ask every new woman I meet what she does and where she works, instead of assuming that she has no separate identity of her own apart from being a Mrs.

So, the next time you are at a party, ensure that you are standing right next to the bar, where people are likely talking about what you are interested in, and not sitting on the sofa in the corner, pretending to discuss shopping. And I am going to make sure that I join you too.

Corporate mantra of the day

- One of the not-so-nice things about being part of a couple is that your partner is always given the primary status, however successful you may be.
- It is important to deal with this stereotyping and make sure that people recognize you as a separate and equally important entity.

Psst...

- Someone has to break up this 'men will stand at the bar and women will discuss shopping on the sofas' parties. Get together with some like-minded women and go and perch on those bar stools!

23

RAISING YOUR HAND
TO SAY 'AYE'

DON'T RUN AWAY TILL YOU
ABSOLUTELY HAVE TO!

I am sitting with my market head and discussing her career plans with her. There is an opportunity that has opened up in our organization and a zonal head vacancy is available for her if she wants to take it. However, this will mean her moving to another city, far away from her parents and family.

'Shweta, I think this will be a great move for you career-wise. It will give you a chance to understand a new market and handle several small regions at the same time. You must take this up,' I tell her. I can't understand why she has not jumped at this chance given that HR offered it to her a week back, so I have called her into my room for a discussion.

'But, ma'am, I'm not sure. It will mean leaving my parents. And a new city...' mumbles Shweta.

'Nonsense! You are thirty-four years old. How long do you plan on staying at home and remaining tied by the umbilical cord? And your parents are quite capable of managing on their own, aren't they? So what's the real problem? Come on, out with it.' I am not convinced by her spiel; I want her to tell me the actual reason.

After a bit of dithering (from her) and jostling (from me) she divulges the real issue. 'No, really, ma'am, I don't want to leave my parents. Also, they are looking for a boy for me. And you know how Punjabi boys are. He will be from a business family, so after marriage I won't be able to move out of the city in any case. And, then, if I have kids? Who will take care of them? So I have to be near my parents for that eventuality too...' she trails off, looking earnestly at me, expecting me to understand.

I am taken aback. We all know that her parents have been looking for a boy for her for quite a while now. It seems to be a constant work-in-progress project—in the five years she has been with us, she (or her parents) haven't yet found anyone suitable. In fact, I have been under the impression that even now there is no prospective candidate anywhere in their immediate vicinity; but perhaps things have progressed further on that front than I know of.

'So, have you met someone?' I plod on to figure out if the appearance of a Mr Shweta on the horizon is imminent. 'Is he a businessman based here?'

'Oh, no, ma'am!' Shweta blushes. 'I am just saying... supposing...'

Supposing? Shweta is ready to throw away a heaven-sent opportunity for an eventuality that may or may not play out in the near future? She is actually tossing away a chance to forge ahead in her career only on the possibility that a day will come in her life when she will need her parents around to babysit. She will be a disastrous bridge player, I think to myself, talk about calculating the odds!

Intelligent and practical otherwise, many women end up making this same mistake. Is it a subconscious fear of flying high? Of achieving so much that she may never be able to find an equal partner? Or is it just the unwillingness of leaving the comfort of the parental nest? Whatever it is, in this curiously reverse case of missing the trees for the woods, Shweta is foregoing a chance to fast-track her career. She is turning down an opportunity that is available to her in the immediate present for a future contingency that may never play out the way she is imagining it.

Nine out of ten times, women make the mistake of moving to the sidelines much before they are asked to do so. They don't seem to realize that eventually there will come a time when they have no choice but to jump off their gravy train, at least for a while. A few years of their lives will have to be dedicated to the process of childbearing and their careers will necessarily have to take a backseat. It is a challenge they have to contend with anyway—why not make the most of all possibilities before that?

In Shweta's case, since there is no immediate groom on the horizon, the time when she will have to step back in her career is many years away. But she has already decided to take a backseat. And a process that could have been contained to a fewer number of years is going to spread out over a much larger part of her career. We will have no choice but to offer the role to her male colleague instead, an employee who is already straining at the leash and will jump at this chance for career advancement, uprooting himself along with his family to move to a new city. I can see his career already moving into the next trajectory, whereas poor Shweta has wilfully embraced the slower path. Not because the organization obstructed her growth but because she chosen to let go of the opportunity.

Each time this kind of break comes along, or an option arises to participate in a project that may involve travel or late nights or working on weekends, I see far more male hands go up than women's hands. I can almost see the wheels churning in the minds of women when I ask for participation in these projects. 'How will I cope? This will mean reaching home late every day for the next two weeks. Who will prepare Bunty's dinner? And Bhabhi is coming over with her kids next week, I'll have to manage that too... Better to say no.'

They don't seem to realize that by turning down this opportunity, and the next, and the next, they will also end up losing the battle for the next promotion.

A few of the women will blame the organization for discrimination; some will understand that they themselves chose to compromise on their careers; many will simply give up and leave. Regardless, the ultimate loser, unfortunately, is going to be the woman herself.

As we climb the rungs of success, we have to realize that we have no other recourse but to put up our hands and accept the opportunities organizations give us—training workshops, the scope for learning new skills, special projects, new growth paths, and so on. We have to try and restrict the times we say no to only those crucial years when we have no choice, when our kids are small, or when our ailing parents desperately need our help.

At any other time, saying no is a luxury we just can't afford. Because every nay is a step backwards in our careers, and so many brakes applied at so many junctures can only harm the engine. Especially when that long childbearing halt is looming ahead and has already been pre-written into our route plan by virtue of being a woman.

CORPORATE MANTRA OF THE DAY

- Women start preparing for marriage and motherhood far earlier than they need to. In the process, the period when they step back from their careers lasts much longer than required, compromising their professional growth.
- Good organizations typically don't discriminate against their female employees. Don't blame the organization for the choices you made along the way.

PSST...

- Special projects are the organization's way of checking whether you are ready for the next role—never say no to them!

24

YOUR MALE SUBORDINATES ARE WIRED DIFFERENTLY, POOR THINGS!

DEALING WITH MALE JUNIORS

If you have scaled the ladder of achievement and reached so far, it is natural to assume that you will have at various junctures led a team, a department, or even your own organization as the captain of the ship. It would also be very much in the scheme of things to assume that a large percentage of your team has been of the male species.

So, how do you deal with your male subordinates? Do you treat them the same as you do your female underlings? Better? Worse? Or are you one of those bosses who cannot even distinguish whether a person is male or female, and even if you could you wouldn't give a damn anyway? Is, according to you, everyone around you a machine meant to do your bidding and nothing else?

Well, here's a secret which I need to share with you. Just as reams have been written about the female co-worker and how to deal with her, because all bosses up until now have been largely male and most of them don't understand the female mind, the time has come to now educate the female boss on how to deal with and get work out of her male junior.

For instance, if I want something done by any of my female team members, all I need to do is simply walk up to her and directly tell her to do so. 'Malini, I was just thinking that, instead of going to the client with a straight FCT option, let's offer them a package of FCT and also some on-ground events.' FCT (Fixed Commercial Time) is the advertising time that all TV and radio channels sell to advertisers to earn their livelihood and feed their families. Because it is a sensible suggestion, Malini's response to it will be a simple yes and she will immediately start working on the best package for the client.

However, I just cannot do something as simple as that with one of my male juniors. Indeed, if I suggest something to him, he will immediately have a counter-argument ready, or an objection, or an intelligent-sounding reason for why it is not possible to integrate events into the FCT package. And we will spend hours having mind-numbing discussions about the same thing. Simply because he has to demonstrate that he is in control all the time, and accepting any suggestion from the boss will demonstrate that he is not in control.

So, I have to play it slightly differently.

'Hey, Amit, how are things going? And how's your client behaving?' I accost Amit in the corridor and insidiously start the process of getting him to do what I want.

Amit then launches into a five-minute spiel about how his client is so difficult but how he himself is so great that he has tackled all the issues splendidly and is now completely in control of everything.

I nod my head admiringly and then surreptitiously slide

the point I want to make into the conversation: 'By the way, I was wondering if there is any way to excite the client into spending more? I am not sure how to do it. Maybe a package? I hear he likes events…'

And then I quickly exit the stage before he has a chance to reply (to evade the inevitable objections/counter-arguments, etc., mentioned previously). My job here is to sow the seed and move on. Sometimes, it takes a few days to germinate. Sometimes, if the boy is bright, it can be as soon as a couple of hours.

Sure enough, Amit comes bouncing into my room the very next day. 'Boss, I have cracked it. I have a great idea to make the client spend more. Let's give him a package of spots and events. I know I will be able to convince him,' he exclaims excitedly, looking thoroughly pleased with himself, like a puppy who has just laid down a juicy bone before his master. He gazes at me expectantly waiting, for my approbation.

'Wow, what innovative thinking, Amit, well done! Now let's go for it.' A seasoned handler of men by now, I respond instantly, without a moment's hesitation.

Amit leaves my room, his tail wagging, and I know the job will be done flawlessly.

The end always justifies the means, don't you think? If I had told him directly, I would have had to struggle for several hours because Amit would have wanted to prove that his point was right—rather, that my point was wrong.

I have learnt long ago that, in the case of the male ego, it is not about what works and delivers results but that he should always be right and everyone else wrong. As far as his territory is concerned, he must always be seen to know best, and nobody should be able tell him better.

The big secret in male subordinate management, therefore, is to always make him believe that whatever he is doing is of his own volition. The strategy is his, the ideas are his and the way he deals with work is also his choice.

While with a woman you can instruct and direct, with a man you have to subtly suggest (and the more subliminal the suggestion the better it works). I would love it if I could discover the trick of apparating into my male subordinates' dreams and defining their tasks for them for the next day. I am sure they would get up and do exactly as I wanted, all the while believing that they have thought of it all on their own. I would then not need to waste any time at all in the circuitous deviations I have to do to get them to work as per my expectations.

'Karan, the two critical things that ensure the success of our radio station is the music we play and the topicality of what the RJs speak.'

While conducting the induction of a new programming head, I spent time explaining to him what made us tick at our radio station. Since he was new and had moved from television to work with us, he vigorously nodded his head. I knew that nothing I was saying was penetrating into his brain, but since it was his first day he was pretending to listen. Over the next few months, I tried and told him the same thing in various different ways. I asked him to research the music we played, I asked him to get the RJs to read the newspapers every day and then use current news items as talking points on air.

But Karan was on an alternate path of his own thinking. He spent more time on creating pre-produced shows than on music. The RJs' source of information switched to Facebook rather than to newspapers (which, in any case, they abhorred) and they sounded even more inane as a consequence.

A firm believer in letting people learn from their own mistakes, I was loath to interfere, and Karan was doing a good job otherwise of getting the team aligned and creating some great on-air content. But my patience had started wearing thin when he walked up to me one day and grandly announced, 'Boss, I had an epiphany last night! I want to share it with you when you have some time.'

He came into my cabin at the designated time with a full-fledged PowerPoint presentation that he turned on with a flourish. The first slide appeared in bedazzling colours, and the headline floated in: 'A RADIO STATION IS ONLY AS GOOD AS THE MUSIC IT PLAYS!'

I was stunned. I looked at him in speechless amazement.

Pleased with the effect he had caused (and misunderstanding the reason for my speechlessness), Karan carries on. 'Boss did you know that 90% of our content is music? And that the most successful stations in the world are those who have researched every piece of music they play on air?'

I bit my tongue to prevent myself from asking him why he was replaying my thoughts back to me.

Blissfully oblivious to the acerbic comments rampaging through my mind, he said, 'This completely changes things, you see. I don't know why we are concentrating on pre-produced shows so much and wasting our time. If you take my advice, we should immediately start reviewing our playlists. And please allow me to order all the morning newspapers so that the RJs can read them.' He closed his laptop with a snap.

I nodded my head ironically and he walked triumphantly out of the room, believing he had made his point decisively and clearly. I could see him standing outside my cabin, regaling his juniors with the effect his incisive strategy had on me, and how it had left me thunderstruck with awe and admiration.

I wanted to call him back and scream: 'What the hell have I been telling you for the last three months? And now you have the effrontery to walk up to me and tell me YOU have figured out that music is very important? And, to make matters worse, you behave as if it's a great insight that you just got?'

But I am a wise boss (seriously!). I realize that if people feel that the ideas are theirs they will execute them much better. And so I let Karan feel thrilled with himself and his newfound acumen. After all, ultimately, the benefit was going to accrue to the organization, so how did it matter?

As women bosses, let us not make the mistake erstwhile male bosses made—of not understanding what made their female juniors tick. Yet another sign of our superiority will be if we can be better managers of both sexes.

CORPORATE MANTRA OF THE DAY

- Male and female subordinates have different buttons and need to be handled differently.
- While women can be told directly or instructed since they won't make it an ego issue, men have to be managed more artfully, by allowing them to believe that they are in full control of their destinies.

PSST...

- As long as you get your work done, it doesn't really matter who gets the credit for the ideas. You are not in competition with anyone, especially your juniors, so let them believe they think up the strategies—they will work harder.

25

CHANGING THE STATUS QUO SINGLE-HANDEDLY

SEXY, SMART AND SINGLE

While we are on the topic of achievement: one of the strongest testimonies to the fact that women have truly started conquering the world is the number of successful single women we see around us today.

Notwithstanding the horrid tags that people attach to them (the most recent one being 'sheng-nu', which in Chinese means 'leftover' woman and suggests that any woman above the age of twenty-seven is way past her sell-by date), the single woman today is skilfully navigating her life all by herself out of choice, and on her own terms. She packs her bags and relocates to a new city in search of better prospects without blinking an eyelid at the attendant woes of searching for a new house, gas connection and cook. She dashes off at a moment's notice to the newest tourist hotspot with just her camera for company, not worrying about real or imagined problems single women could face while travelling. She unilaterally takes decisions on career choices, on the new car to buy and the investments she wants to make. She neither needs help in changing the light bulb nor in reaching the airport at 3.30 in the morning.

Obviously, navigating the treacherous corridors of singledom, especially in countries such as ours, is not easy. It is very irritating to deal with the pesky landlord who wants to have 'discussions' about the rent with her late in the evening just because she is single. It is equally frustrating to be stopped by cops who want to know why she is driving alone so late in the night. It is exasperating answering both the nosy aunt at the wedding and the nosy lady in the train seat next to her as to why she is not married and whether or not she is worried about her biological clock ticking away. But I see her valiantly handling these challenges as she goes about charting her own path, chugging along on her own steam, everywhere I look around in India today.

'Arey, Nimmi beta, I didn't see you at the engagement yesterday? How are you?' Pammi Aunty asks my cousin Nirmala as she waddles up to us, saccharine sweet as always.

Nirmala is standing next to me with a face as black as a thundercloud because I have forced her to come with me for our mutual cousin's wedding. She had refused to come to the engagement the previous day citing work as an excuse, but I knew that for the last couple of years she had completely stopped attending family get-togethers simply because she was fed up of the constant scrutiny and discussions about her unmarried status. However, for the wedding, I had ignored her pleas and literally dragged her out of the house—which is why she is standing next to me, glowering.

'I am fine, Aunty, and what about you?' Plastering a fake smile on her face, Nimmi says in response.

'Oh, I am very well. Became a granny for the second time. You girls must have heard that Shilpa had a baby last month?' Pammi Aunty beams proudly.

'Of course we did. Congratulations, Aunty!' we chorus at her.

'And what about you Nimmi? Still single? Beta, why don't you find a good guy and get married now? This is not good, you know, to be alone. After all, Shilpa and you are the same age. And see where she has reached... Two little angels and a lovely family...' Pammi Aunty launches into attack mode without any preliminaries.

'And also a lovely thirty-six-inch waist to go with the lovely family,' I mutter sotto voce. Out loud, I proclaim: 'But, Aunty, where is the time for her to get married? Didn't you hear? Nimmi was made vice president of her company this year and she is just so busy... Travelling all around the world. London, Paris, New York...' I defend my favourite cousin loyally while she stands next to me radiating waves of wrath.

'Hmm. And is that going to take care of her in her old age? With no husband and kids to support her?' Pammi Aunty sniffs disparagingly. 'And...'

Thankfully, at this point, one of her little angels comes running to her, shrieking 'Nani', and she moves off.

Nimmi furiously pulls me to a corner. 'I told you not to bring me with you. All these old biddies will now pile on to me.'

'Relax, Nimmi. Just ignore them, yaar. Chal, there's the chaat counter... Let's go and have some pani puri. I know it's your favourite.' I drag her along with me and we spend the next half hour blissfully gorging ourselves on the various chaat options that are such an integral part of a Punju wedding.

'Oye, Nimmi, Nimmi!' calls out a piercing voice behind us.

'Oh, no!' We groan in unison.

It is Dolly Aunty, our extended family's official matchmaker and agony aunt par excellence. She has been actively pursuing Nimmi and looks at her as one of her few failures. Someone had overheard her saying once that she wouldn't die in peace till she ensured that Nimmi got married—she apparently owed it to Nimmi's parents, who were two of the first people she had matched.

'I didn't realize you would be here, child, otherwise I would have come and met you earlier.' Dolly Aunty beams at Nimmi. 'I have been meaning to call you since yesterday. I have found just the boy for you, Nimmi Rani! He is a manager in a bank. And not one of those nasty foreign banks, let me tell you, but our very own Punjab Bank. Can you believe it? He's at a very high post too. The whole of the Andheri branch reports to him, I believe. He's just moved to Mumbai from Ludhiana and he's living all alone, poor thing. His mother called me up the other day and told me to find a girl for him immediately. She told me tearfully, "I am putting my child in your hands, Dolly. Find a girl for him. How will he manage alone? Who will cook for him?"'

We burst into fits of laughter. Nimmi cooking for someone? Nimmi, who was famous as a master chef specializing in one dish alone? Scrambled eggs? (With minor variations such as with or without onions, with or without Tabasco sauce, with or without burnt toast, and so on.) Hah! And hah again.

Dolly Aunty looks affronted. 'Really, I don't know what there is to laugh about. Acchha, tell me, when shall I fix up for the two of you to meet?'

'But have you checked with his mother whether she is okay with a bahu who can't cook and smokes and drinks once in a while?' I tease Aunty. 'And what about the mismatch between their salaries? There is bound to be at least a few zeros' difference. Will a Punju macho man be able to deal with a wife who earns so much more?'

'At this rate, Nimmi is never going to get married! Where will she find someone who earns more? They all got married long ago.' Aunty glares at us. 'And has she thought about that clock ticking away in her body? What do you call it? That biological-shiological nonsense. Very soon she won't be able to have a baby. Then what? Tell me? Tell me?'

Nimmi by now has had enough. 'Don't worry, Aunty. I have already frozen my eggs. And I have also got in touch with Aamir. As soon as he is free from his next movie, he is going to donate his sperm. Imagine...you will become a great-aunt to Aamir's child!' She smiles sweetly smiles before walking off, nose held high.

Dolly Aunty turns red, blue and purple. 'What nonsense you girls talk!' Huffing, off she walks in the opposite direction.

Unfortunately in India, and elsewhere in Asian countries, being single is still a sort of social stigma. Not only does the single girl have to deal with society looking its nose down at her just because she is not married but she also has to deal with a huge amount of pressure from her family and friends. The guilt of dealing with the worry on her parents' face and the concern of her friends, the frustration of snide comments made by relatives and the loneliness that sometimes hits her when she is all alone on a Saturday night while her friends are busy with their families—it can be quite distressing.

Through all this, however, shines her immense courage in looking life straight in the eye and demanding that it treat her on her own terms. The guts she demonstrates when she cocks a snook at society and says she will only do what is right for her, with no compromises and no settling for what she doesn't believe in, is truly admirable.

I think the single woman today truly epitomizes the success

that women have achieved in taking control of their own destinies and finally becoming mistresses of their fates. May her flag always fly high!

CORPORATE MANTRA OF THE DAY

- If you are out there—alone and bravely running your life exactly as you have chosen to—and sometimes get frustrated and lonely, remember we are all right here, egging you on, admiring you, standing up for you.

PSST...

- Married friends will always try and convince you that the grass on their side is greener, but I am sure there is a hint of envy when they see the freedom you have. And don't think you are alone. There are many women just like you, marching along to a beat only they can hear. Enjoy!

26

BRICKS AND STONES WILL NOT BREAK MY BONES

STONE AGE MEN

I bumped into a batch mate after twenty-odd years at the crowded lounge of the Delhi airport. In a large herd of self-important males who studied with me at the Indian Institute of Management, he was the king beast. After the usual exchange of pleasantries, and him portentously informing me that he was Head of Sales of a Tractor Company in Hissar (he had the habit of speaking about himself in Capital letters, even back in our student days), the conversation went something like this.

He: 'I have been following your career quite closely over the years, you know.'

Me: Polite fixed smile.

He: 'I believe you were heading Zee TV and then started Zoom TV, and now you are the CEO of Radio City. See, I know everything about you.' Smiling indulgently at me.

Me: Polite smile getting even more rigid. (I didn't know

how to react since I couldn't, for the life of me, figure out where this conversation was heading.)

He: 'So, tell me, do you work full-time or part-time?'

I goggled and gasped. (As you can see, I do loads of goggling and gasping, especially when I meet strange men.) I didn't know whether I should laugh or cry or slap him hard. Have you ever heard of a part-time CEO? Or even a part-time sales head or marketing head? Is it possible? How the hell did he think I was running such a large organization? From my kitty party? Or on Mondays, Wednesdays and Fridays, when I didn't have yoga class?

I was immediately transported two decades back, to campus, which was the only time and place on earth that I have faced gender bias of any nature. As one of the ten women in a batch of 120 students, I remember always feeling like an insect under a microscope. In that highly competitive environment, we were subtly made to feel that, by virtue of being female, we were already a notch inferior to the rest of the students there.

Fortunately, in the last twenty-three years of working, I have never faced that type of bias ever again. Maybe it comes out of being part of an industry which has traditionally had a larger number of women employees. Or maybe I have just been fortunate to work with some great people. Or maybe I have never given out or received any vibes that say: 'Come, let's play some sexy games with each other.'

As we climb the ladder of success, on several occasions we will encounter people like the Stone Age Man from Hissar, who despite graduating from one of the premier institutes of the country continues to believe that working women are in office for light amusement, while men are out there doing all the important work, like selling tractors.

At the other end of the spectrum, we will also meet fierce

feminists who want to make-believe that the only reason men walk the earth is to cause the ruin of women, and that most of them are lurking stealthily in every corridor and doorway with the sole purpose of attacking any woman who passes by.

While this in no fashion is meant to point fingers at or demean any woman who has faced the horrors of sexual harassment or gender bias in her life, I also feel that some ardent feminists take the whole bias thing to an extreme level.

At one of the organizations I worked for, I was the senior-most female staff member, and as such was perpetually being invited to be part of various panel discussions for which the organization deemed it fit to have a female representative. I am always happy to go share my views with whomever cares to listen (that's the only thing CEOs do, if you haven't figured it out by now). In one particular case, however, I firmly refused to go for a discussion since it was going to revolve around sexual harassment at the workplace, and how to deal with it. Having never faced it myself and not knowing anyone who had been a victim, I said to the lady organizing the conference that I wouldn't know what to say.

She was aghast. 'How can you say that?' She glared at me with an accusing look on her face.

'But it's true,' I responded, startled by her vehemence.

'That's probably because you have always been in a powerful position. How would you ever understand? It's the more vulnerable women at junior levels who face this trauma!' Her lips quivered in indignation.

'Well, I haven't always been in this position, you know. I too started at the bottom of the ladder as a trainee, and I didn't face this sort of trouble anywhere,' I retorted sharply, stung by the condemnation in her tone.

'Maybe you don't understand what constitutes sexual

harassment then,' she said scornfully. 'Every time a guy tells you "Hey, you are looking good!" Or calls you "sweetheart". That's sexual harassment too.'

I burst out laughing. I just could not help myself—she was so earnest and yet so foolish. 'If that is the case, there are going to be sexual harassment cases against me then. I have called all the boys who reported to me "Raja" at some point or the other, and have often complimented them if I thought they were looking good.' So saying, I walked away from Ms Hypersensitive.

Both Stone Age Man and Ms Fierce Feminist are extremists and in my mind, too regressive when reality is far more moderate and modern than they imagine.

The contemporary woman is slowly waking up to the fact that while guarding women's rights and respect by being hyper-vigilant was critical in the initial days of breaking the glass ceiling, today she doesn't need to be suspicious of every male and take umbrage at every light-hearted comment he makes.

I know that many women do get disturbed at the condescending way they are treated by men sometimes. My advice is that, as we bump into these sanctimonious gentlemen on our way up, we should treat them with the disdain they deserve, completely ignoring their opinions instead of giving them undue importance with our anger. Haven't we, after all, reached such levels of achievement that we can actually look down on all of these fundamentalists and crush them (metaphorically) with the heels of our stilettos?

For example, when various politicians/college principals/ police chiefs periodically crawl out from under some stone to pass judgement on women and what they should eat and drink (definitely not meat and liquor), where they should be seen (most certainly not bars and clubs) and what they should wear (preferably burqas), various women's organizations take to the streets in protest—this, I feel, is completely the wrong strategy and response.

Personally, I think we should pay no attention to these ridiculous comments. Rather, it should be men's organizations raising their voice against these deeply insulting comments. After all, these comments are far more offensive to men than they are to women. Because they club all men together into a herd of boors who can't control their baser instincts, and at the drop of a hat—rather, at the sight of some skin—start attacking women.

Now, most of the men I know are decent, God-fearing blokes, quietly going about the daily business of earning a living, taking care of their families and praying that Sachin scores his next hundred and never retires. And I am pretty sure that most of your male acquaintances fall in this category too. It is, therefore, far more demeaning for them to be treated as if every action of theirs is governed by lust and they lose all good sense at the sight of a short skirt.

If the keepers of our morality do believe that men, poor things, just can't control themselves, then they should be spending their time more usefully in figuring out how to subdue the male libido rather than pointing fingers at women. I would recommend that they actively look at launching a male chastity belt, a bit like the protective guards our cricketers wear—you know, the ones they keep adjusting in that yucky manner. I am sure that with firmly locked guards we will be able to shield the male population from falling prey to temptation. Imagine if someone had had the bright idea of tying Adam's hands—he wouldn't have reached for the apple, and we would all be living in heavenly bliss.

With the garb of success firmly cloaking us, let us pledge that we will not let either regressive men or super-sensitive women bother us, and we will continue single-mindedly along the path we have charted for ourselves.

CORPORATE MANTRA OF THE DAY

- While women have taken giant strides, both in thinking and in deed, many men are still living in the Stone Age. There is no point in letting their comments bother us.

PSST...

- By making out that women are seductresses and temptresses and men unwilling victims, men end up demeaning their own ilk.

27

WE DON'T NEED NO RESERVATIONS

WELL-DEVELOPED CHESTS WANTED

When I saw the headline 'Well-developed Chests Wanted' emblazoned across the pages of a national daily, I thought to myself: omigosh, the cat is finally out of the bag. An anthropological fact I have long suspected has finally been unveiled by some research or survey. That Indian men have a fixation for the upper parts of a woman's body, brought up as they are on a steady diet of Nirupa Roy clasping Amitabh Bachchan to her bosom amidst poignant cries of 'Beta', is a fact many of us have long been privy to. But to have this stated so openly and in such a public manner, almost like the undergarments you see flying merrily in the windows of DDA flats, startled me quite a bit.

Closer inspection of the article revealed the true story, which was no less startling in its strangeness. Apparently, the Ministry of Home Affairs had recently issued a circular outlining the parameters of selection for women in the Border

Security Force (BSF). And one of these parameters was the need for women applicants to have well-developed chests. Now, the question this automatically begs is: what exactly was the ministry thinking when they outlined this regulation, and what did they expect to do in the BSF with women so endowed? My mind boggled at some of the more creative answers that appeared in my fertile imagination.

On further examination, it was revealed that the ministry had actually circulated the same regulations that were being used for selecting male candidates in the case of female applicants too. And thus the above requirement! It took a parliamentary committee to censure the ministry and ask them to review all recruitment rules and see that there was no derogatory language used regarding women. But, as usual, the bureaucrats missed the woods for the trees.

It is not only a question of language—it is a much larger issue. While we are all laying down gender inclusion policies sitting in our cosy cabins, are we also making enough changes on the ground to accommodate women in the newer workplaces they are so bravely venturing into? For example, has the BSF ensured the suitability of the quarters they assign to women in the force? When they go out on duty, is there infrastructure to take care of the specific requirements they may have?

One lady told me how she has to go to the Port Authorities offices for regular meetings, and there are no loos for women at the docks. And she has day-long meetings out there.

One of the biggest reasons for older girls dropping out of schools in rural areas is the lack of toilets. In a crunch, the boys can go out to the fields; but what will the girls do?

This lack of thinking in what exactly will help women succeed in the workplace was visible once again in an announcement made by the authorities in the fair city of

Gurgaon. (I wonder if we can call it a city, considering that most of its denizens still behave like they live in the jungle?) It was decided that malls and other workplaces should not allow women to work beyond 8 p.m. because they (the authorities, that is) could not guarantee the safety of these women as they travelled home after work. Presumably, the several wolves-dressed-up-in-men's-clothing roaming on the roads would be on the lookout for prey after 8 p.m., and it was deemed more prudent to lock up the cheese than to do anything about the mice. (Pardon the confusing zoological references).

Nobody, of course, gave a moment's thought to the fact that given this diktat many employers would think twice before hiring women and, consequently, women would now find it doubly hard to find jobs. Stretched further, this logic foretells a horrifying future for women: where, as men become increasingly uncontrollable by continuing to remain unchecked and unpunished, more restrictions are put on women. And thus the day may not be very far when these authorities start telling women to remain locked up at home; and if they indeed have to venture out, that they must do so wearing a burqa or under armed escort.

The directive was apparently withdrawn later, but the fact that it was made in the first place is testament enough to the total lack of understanding of the powers-that-be of women's issues in the workplace.

In fact, whenever inclusiveness is discussed in any public sphere, it becomes apparent that either there is complete ignorance about the real issues that women have to deal with in trying to work outside their homes, or it is mere lip service to the entire issue of gender diversity.

For instance, there was the story of a woman commander in a commercial airline getting promoted out of turn (and merit) to meet some diversity target and causing harm to a plane while making a poor landing. Apparently, she was not experienced enough but got promoted quickly ahead of a Women's Day celebration.

I don't know the extent of veracity of this particular story, but I strongly believe that token promotions and reservation targets create more harm than good in the long run. If indeed the story is true, imagine how difficult it will now be for women commanders who are as qualified and as meritorious as their male counterparts to get promoted with this example in front of them. Diversity is a key success driver of business results—by promoting incompetent women simply to fulfil some reservation quota, we will only end up invalidating this premise.

My simple request to all the powers-that-be, therefore, is: please let us be; we don't need your help, your reservations or support to get ahead. We will make it (and, indeed, are making it) on our own steam. However, if you could divert your energy to providing infrastructure which makes travelling at night safe for us, we will be very grateful.

In the meantime, dear men (in case you are reading this—and I hope, for the sake of your own betterment, that you are), your secret is safe with me. I am glad to tell you that no researcher has as yet discovered the truth about what you really thought of all those evocative mother-son scenes in *Deewar*, *Mother India*, *Suhaag* and *Shakti*.

CORPORATE MANTRA OF THE DAY

- There is a lot of debate around reservations and the necessity of using them to help women overcome their current state of backwardness. Mostly, reservation is just tokenism and, in my opinion, will end up harming the cause of women in the long run.

- Solving basic problems, especially in the area of infrastructural support and safety for women, will be far more useful than reservations to ensure their advancement in the workplace.

Psst...

- If by chance you are one of the women who has benefited in some form or another from reservations, make sure that you do the best job you can so that more women are given the same opportunity. Please, for the sake of the sisterhood, don't mess it up.

28

'MEN'TORING FUTURE GENERATIONS

OF CUTE BOYS AND STUDS

I was once invited to judge a fashion show where, hold your hearts, the models were male CXOs! It was a very well conducted, classy event and there were in the all-female panel of judges an ex-Miss India and a celebrity fashion designer, along with me. So it was a fairly diverse spectrum evaluating the contestants—from young to middle-aged, from gorgeous nymphet to aunty, from fashionista to corporate executive.

The participants too were very sporting and an interesting mix of men: tall, dark and handsome; roly-poly and avuncular; clean-shaven boy-next-door; smouldering and mysterious; and flamboyant studs—you know the type, bandana and long hair, blowing kisses to the audience, working hard to create the 'I am a badass' vibe.

We finished judging all the rounds—the formal round, the casual/sporty round and the question-answer round (thankfully, there was no swimwear round; the average male body is not exactly a thing of beauty and a joy forever, after all). We then put our heads together to total up the points and decide on the results. Given my fairly conservative background and my deeply maternal approach (ahem!) to the entire proceedings, I naturally gave the highest points to the 'good, clean, decent boys'.

Much to my shock and surprise, the other two women also gave high points to exactly the same types. Indeed, there was complete consensus on the results and we were ready to announce the winners in matter of minutes. Given the fact that all three of us were from such different backgrounds, profiles and sensibilities, I was quite taken aback with the unanimity of opinion in choosing the same type of male.

Researchers (and romance novel authors) may continue to believe that most women like studs or intense, brooding men with a deep, dark and murky past, but that day I actually got empirical evidence to prove that the womanly heart beats for the cute and decent boy next door! Indeed, the suitable-boy-who-could-be-taken-home-to-be-showcased-proudly-to-parents won hands down over the bad-boy-fit-only-to-be-a-thrilling-boyfriend-and-unsuitable-in-all-other-respects.

As mothers and sisters, therefore, I think it becomes our bounden duty to ensure that we groom and train our sons and brothers to be 'good boys' so that their appeal to the female target segment only goes up. Let's face it, sooner rather than later in countries such as ours, with the gender ratio as skewed as it is, women will form a rare species. It, therefore, behoves us to make sure that we make our sons as attractive marriage partners as possible, so that they are not left on the shelf when their time comes to venture out into the matrimonial market.

In fact, educating the newer generations of males on treating women as equal partners and colleagues, with esteem and respect, should be the key agenda of all senior women today. Whenever people ask me about my views on mentoring, I always answer that mentoring is something we need to do with men rather than women. They are the ones who will need to be sensitized to women if we have any hope of building an equal world for both. I thank my mother-in-law every day for teaching these values to HD when he was a kid. The reason I have such a supportive spouse is because of his upbringing. Will our daughters-in-law say the same about us, I wonder?

A spoilt boy is going to grow up to be a spoilt man. A male child who is used to having his mother, sister and aunt dance attendance on him will expect the same out of his wife and daughter. A boy who has seen his father treat his mother with disrespect will do the same to his wife. It is up to us to ensure that we do not allow this cycle to perpetuate, and cut the loop immediately.

My son is turning out to be an accomplished cook, extremely independent as a person and with no hang-ups about women and their equal place under the sky, mainly because of growing up in an environment where he has only seen complete equality between the sexes in his family.

Back from an overnight stay with one of his friends when he was around eight years old, Sid walked up and with complete innocence asked me, 'You know, Mihir's mother calls his father "aap" and "ji" all the time and serves him tea in his bed every morning. Why does she behave as if he is her boss?'

HD, of course, was greatly amused by Sid's shock at this servile behaviour on the part of Mihir's mother and decided to make a joke out of it and confuse him even further by telling him that in normal families the father typically was the boss, and unfortunately in our household things were very different since I had been mistreating him for years by being a cruel and abnormal wife.

But I was rather pleased by Sid's puzzlement. It said to me that he had only seen the world through the lens of male-female equality until that time—and I was going to make damned sure that this version continued to be his reality for all times to come.

Having spent such a lot of time with several women colleagues and subordinates, the male HODs in our organization have become so sensitive to female issues that they joke that they too suffer from sympathetic PMS in tandem with us. But I have seen them counsel their female juniors on issues ranging from the best way to feed a newborn baby to how to handle school admissions and an irascible father-in-law, with aplomb and immense thoughtfulness.

An important responsibility of being a woman achiever is mentoring the next generation of men so that they grow up to treat women with respect. I, therefore, exhort all you mothers to bring up your sons to treat women as equals, so that the next generation of women don't have to contend with the same issues you did—and you may just have a grateful daughter-in-law writing a memoir in praise of you, as I am doing!

And all the guys who are (hopefully) reading this, my message to you is: throw away those leather jackets and the knuckle busters and erase those tattoos. Trim your hair short and get rid of all that facial fuzz, bathe and shave every day. And definitely listen to your mothers. For, it is a fact that good boys will always finish first.

CORPORATE MANTRA OF THE DAY

- An important responsibility of being a woman achiever is mentoring the next generation of men so that they grow up to respect and treat women as equals. How you behave as a mother and a sister will impact a whole generation of men and, by association, the women they deal with.

Psst...

- Win the heart of your prospective daughter-in-law in advance by training your son to cook, help in the housework and pick up his towel!

29

BUILDING A REPUTATION, NOT A CV

WHAT WILL PEOPLE SAY ABOUT YOU TWENTY YEARS LATER?

'Ik baar waqt se lamha gira kahin, wahan daastan banee, lamha kahin nahin.'

These are Gulzar's lyrics from the song 'Aane wala pal' in the movie *Golmaal*. As only he can, he evocatively paints a picture of a moment dropping out of time and leaving behind a story that has been created in that instant.

In all our lives, there are several such moments that trigger a chain of events none of us can foretell or foresee. They come and go like grains of sand slipping through our fingers, and none of us can anticipate the exact moment which has the power to subsequently alter our lives. I remember an episode in my life whose after-effects I felt much later, and which ended up affecting my career quite dramatically.

Many years back, HD and I had moved to Chennai when he changed his job. I got a job with the advertising firm I had worked for earlier, but the role was not meaty or exciting enough compared to what I had been doing in Mumbai. It kept me busy for half the day; after that, I had precious little to do. No one was watching me, so I could have easily had a relaxed life at work. As long as I finished the limited work I had, I could have spent that one year enjoying myself, leading a comfortable and cushy existence. But not having been born into an aristocratic family, that particular lifestyle didn't exactly appeal to me. So I started doing any extra work that I could lay my hands on. A monthly newsletter here, some analysis for another department there, and so on.

Word spread across the agency's other branches that there was this extra-eager beaver in the Chennai branch, who would churn out presentations and analyses for whoever wanted them—soon, all the extra work that no one had time to do was getting dumped on me. The new president of the company realized what was happening, and soon I was handling all new business pitches that the agency was making and, as such, coming into direct contact with him all the time. He was a very dynamic person and a man in a hurry to win as many businesses as possible, so we were soon doing a pitch a week and working at a feverish pace.

One day I got a call from his office. 'There is an urgent pitch presentation in Bangalore the day after tomorrow. You need to be there for it.'

'But I have malaria,' I informed them, having been diagnosed just that morning.

'Oh. But Sanjeev Sir is travelling, so I can't get in touch with him. You will have to figure out a way. I have been only told to pass on this message to you.' So saying, the disembodied voice floated away.

Burning with fever, browbeaten by an aching head and reeling under the effects of a strong dose of quinine, I booked my tickets and reached the venue for the presentation on the designated day. Holding myself together with only sheer will power, I stood up and made the presentation and then caught the earliest flight back. Only then did I allow myself to fall ill properly and remained in bed till the fever abated.

We didn't win the account, and life moved on. I forgot the incident, and a year later HD and I moved back to Mumbai. Along with that shift, I rejoined my earlier workplace and organization.

A few years later, I got a call from Sanjeev, who had now become the group CEO of a very large media network, offering me a job that catapulted me straightaway into the big leagues. 'I have rarely seen such work ethic like you exhibited in Chennai, and I want you in my team,' he said while handing me my appointment letter.

Most of us don't work with the specific perspective that we are out there to impress our bosses. We work hard because that's our job and our internal moral compass drives us to do so. And that's exactly what I was doing in Chennai. Frankly, I hadn't even imagined that my path would ever cross Sanjeev's in the future, let alone that he would end up heading a big media outfit and call me to work with him there.

But we also have to realize that there are points in our lives where, unknown to us, we will be under close scrutiny. And which is the moment that will turn out to be the decisive one in making (or marring) our fortunes is something we will realize only much later on.

Therefore, the only way to behave is to treat every moment of our lives as preciously as possible. Each day at work, we need to conduct ourselves with as much diligence and sincerity as possible. Every moment has to matter to us and make a difference, big or small, to the environment around us.

And whilst we are doing that, unknown to us, our

reputation is getting created. Our colleagues, our bosses, our clients, even the casually met supplier, are building or marring our reputation—so, ten years down the line people will either say 'Oh, she is a great worker; she is tough but a good people manager, she knows her job' or 'She is a bit of a shirker and needs to be pushed; too many people problems, ethics issues and so on'.

At that stage, it will be too late to do anything because none of us have the ability to go back in time and change the way we behaved. And we will end up becoming creations of the choices we made along the way, of working hard or not, of fudging the expense statement or not, of being nasty with people or not.

The truth is that a good reputation cannot be created in a day or rewritten on expensive paper. The flaws cannot be air-brushed and spruced up. A good reputation has to be assiduously built, over millions of moments of being diligent, sincere, hardworking and ethical.

And when the big break comes our way, of the CXO position or the willingness of the fund-house to invest in our business, a fancy CV will not help. What will matter is the reputation we have built and what people are saying about us as professionals.

Therefore, let us remember that, while we are hurrying along in our journey to excel, we must ensure that we make every moment count and add to our reputation and not detract from it.

CORPORATE MANTRA OF THE DAY

- In our quest to build an impressive CV, we sometimes forget that what is more important is our reputation.
- A good reputation cannot be created in a day or

rewritten on paper, unlike a CV. It is built over millions of moments of being diligent, sincere, hardworking and ethical.

Psst..

*   How you behave when no one is supervising (or when you are serving out your notice period) will define your true worth and the efficacy of your personal moral compass.

30

CHEST-THUMPING IS OKAY

CELEBRATING SUCCESS

The other day, HD and I were sitting together and having coffee. It was one of those relaxed Sunday mornings, a slight chill in the air, silence all around and everything going right with the world. I happened to glance up from the paper and saw him gazing very fondly at me, a loving look in his eyes. Now, after two decades of matrimony, I don't get these looks very often, so you can understand why I immediately perked up.

Preening a bit, I asked him softly, 'What are you thinking of, darling?' I was obviously looking forward to some rare bits of praise or a compliment or something equally pleasant.

HD smiled, sighing reminiscently. 'I was just reflecting on our life and thinking what a wonderfully extraordinary husband I have been all these many years...'

'Excuse me?' I squeaked indignantly, good humour evaporating in a second, 'Wonderful? Extraordinary? Wouldn't you say that is a bit of an exaggeration? You haven't been too bad, I grant you, but this fulsome praise is quite an overkill, if you ask me.' I immediately recalled various instances in the past when he hadn't exactly come up to scratch in the 'great husband' stakes.

But HD was in a pleasant reverie of his own, where no doubt he was up on a stage collecting the 'Husband of the Decade' award.

The fact is that self-praise comes very easily to most men, who are typically born with the belief that they are the greatest thing to have happened to the world. And, as they grow up, they get very little feedback from anyone around to disabuse them of this notion. Women, however, struggle to believe that they are important. Having been told from childhood to be demure, to sit with their legs crossed, to not talk too loudly while their brothers ran rambunctiously around, every cue they have been given is to be invisible and occupy as little space as possible, both physically and mentally, in the family.

So, is it any wonder that we have all heard of the alpha male but no one has yet heard of the alpha female? Simply because she doesn't exist.

Take a look around the plane the next time you travel. Invariably, there will be one of these alpha men around, who make sure that everyone on the flight knows that He is there amidst them, gasp! This alpha male will insist on entering the flight last, with a big bag that he will try to shove into the overhead compartment two sizes too small, all the while talking loudly on the phone and giving dirty looks to the hapless crew members. He will trample over everyone's feet without any apology (after all, he is such a Very, Very Important Person that lowly mortals like us are of no significance to him, let alone our poor feet). He won't have dinner along with the rest of the passengers but will make the crew run around five minutes prior to landing to serve him his meal, because that is the time that is convenient to him. He will switch on his phone the very second the pilot announces touchdown, never mind that it is 1.30 a.m., to check if the world around him has collapsed in the two hours he has been AWOL. Frankly, I suspect these men just call up a random number and start giving instructions loudly to reiterate their VVIP status to the people around them. Which rational employee or wife is likely to be taking instructions at that hour, pray tell me?

I have had the misfortune of getting one of these types as a co-passenger on the majority of my flights, the most recent one being a gentleman called Shamsher. Shamsher clearly thought that he had to live up to his name; thus, for the entire period that mobile phones were allowed on the flight (and for a brief period when they weren't), he ensured that all of us became unwilling participants in his loud discussions with boss, wife, driver, colleague and secretary.

And so we heard how unhappy he was with the rates his subordinates had offered in some deal, how his secretary needed to organize stay and transport for an unfortunate Timothy who had missed his connecting flight, what he wanted cooked for dinner, etc., etc.

Typically, the flight at that late hour is filled with poor corporate souls who have just finished a stressful day running from one meeting to another, mobilizing their troops to achieve the month's target, answering deep questions put to them by their board or sitting in on tortuous negotiations with cynical clients. Therefore, the last thing anyone wants is to share in The Life and Times of Mr Shamsher, however fascinating it may be. Unfortunately, though, none of us could parachute out of the flight, no matter how much we fantasized about doing so.

Now, tell me, have you ever encountered the same problem with a woman passenger?

If you ask a male CEO for the reasons his organization is successful, he will launch into an hour-long lecture on how great he is, what a visionary leader he has been and the various strategies he has developed to counter competition, astounding the market and enthralling his shareholders along the way. The 'I' word will be used abundantly in the conversation.

In contrast, if you ask a woman CEO running an equally successful organization the same question, she will falter, hesitate and then meander into an Oscar-worthy speech, thanking parents, husband, ex-boyfriends and cats for their support, and praising her team, her boss and God and giving credit to everyone except herself for the wonderful job done.

Women simply find it very difficult to say good things about themselves, mostly under the assumption that they will be seen to be bragging if they compliment themselves. While men, of course, believe it is their God-given right to do so. And maybe they are not too wrong in this thinking.

If you go back a stage or two in the evolution of man, when primitive man went out hunting or fighting, he had to make himself look bigger than his prey or his enemy. So a lot of noise, drum-beating, huge feathered headdresses and scarily painted faces were necessary accoutrements. Chest-thumping to show superiority was an important requirement for survival.

In the meantime, the woman was staying back in the cave or tent where she was rearing and nurturing children, along with other women. In that setting and context, working together in harmony was more important than trying to show who the queen bee was. So it was not exactly an imperative to praise herself; indeed, it would have been quite counter-productive.

But things have changed today. As we women take on the hunter's role and go out there in the corporate jungle to fight, we need to equip ourselves to do the job well, including training ourselves to do some of the things that don't come naturally to us but are required if we want to hunt well.

So, ladies, here is the last and final lesson of the day. If you have done something to feel proud of and attained something in life, make sure you talk about it.

You have reached this position by dint of extreme hard work. You have learnt to accept many tough realities about your life and also how to adapt to and make them work for you. You have achieved success by managing to have a great career and an equally fulfilling personal life, without compromising on either. It is time to celebrate this success. Don't shy away from saying good things about yourself, from telling your bosses and shareholders, friends and family what a great woman you truly are!

CORPORATE MANTRA OF THE DAY

- Certainly praise your team and always remember to thank the people who supported you, because that's what good managers do; but also take a few minutes to articulate the good things you yourself did, without being brash. Saying good things about yourself becomes easier if you think of yourself as another member in the team who also needs to be complimented.

PSST...

- Make a promise that, every morning, when you get ready to go to work and are putting on your lipstick and your powder, you will say to yourself: 'I am great!' Because you certainly are.

THE TEN LESSONS OF ACHIEVEMENT

1. **As I step on the ladder of success, I will always remember how lucky I am**

    Very few women in the world have received the benefit of an education and the opportunity of using that education to gain financial independence. Let us continually remember how fortunate we are.

2. **I will assert that I am an individual**

    It is important to deal with and debunk the stereotyping of being thought of only in context of the males in our family, as wife/mother/daughter. We must make sure that people recognize us as separate and equally important entities.

3. **I will not walk away ahead of schedule**

    Women start preparing for marriage and motherhood far earlier than they need to and, in the process, the period when they step back from their careers grows unnecessarily long, compromising their growth. We must avoid this.

4. **As a boss, I will recognize that I have to treat my male subordinates differently**

    Male and female subordinates have different buttons, and need to be handled differently. We must keep this in mind and work accordingly for the success of our projects.

5. **I am proud to be successful, smart and single**

    Successful single women are a critical demonstration of

the freedom women have achieved in taking control of their own destinies. The sisterhood salutes them.

6. **I will not let Stone Age Men or zealots affect me**

    Regressive men and overzealous feminists are polarized ends of a spectrum and can affect women negatively. Always remain a liberal thinker on the climb to the top.

7. **I do not want the crutch of reservation to succeed**

    Reservations tend to be mere tokenism and can actually harm the cause of women in the long run by promoting mediocrity. We should compete on a level playing field and not depend on reservations to succeed.

8. **I will pay my dues to the next generation of women by mentoring the younger men around me**

    An important responsibility of being a woman achiever is mentoring the next generation of men so that they grow up to respect and treat women as equals.

9. **As I whizz up the steps of success, I will always remember that building a good reputation is more important than building a good CV**

    A good reputation cannot be created in a day. It is built over millions of moments of being diligent, sincere, hardworking and ethical.

10. **I will celebrate my success openly and without embarrassment**

    It is important to recognize our achievements and celebrate them. Let us learn something from men for a change and praise ourselves whenever we need to.

EPILOGUE

It is 8 p.m., and I am stuck in a traffic jam on the way back from work. It's been a difficult day and the only thing I want is to get back home as quickly as possible. But obviously the Mumbai traffic cops have a different agenda. Being deeply spiritual souls, they have been blessed with the knowledge that the journey is as important as the final destination and want me to recognize this profound truth. So they have strategized and decided on this particular day and this particular hour to set up nakabandis on the main arterial road from my office to my house.

Having no choice in the matter, I sit back and reflect on the day gone by, specifically the disastrous meeting we had with the bureaucrats today. The entire industry has been lobbying the government for the last three years to ease some restrictions on FM radio and make it on par with other media. We finally thought we would see light at the end of the long, dark tunnel, with the hope that some sanctions would come our way, but the bureaucrats have yet again delayed the policy—for the fifth time, citing some internal approvals they have not got. No wonder the country is in the state it is, I think to myself bitterly.

The call with the investors had gone well, though, and the regional head who had quit has decided to stay back. At least something good happened today, I say to myself. The HR head and I had to spend a couple of hours with the regional head trying to get to the bottom of his sudden decision and figuring out how we could change his mind, and we managed to convince him in the end. It seems his wife thought that he should have got a promotion this time and had been pestering him to prove his manhood by quitting—even though he didn't want to leave. Of course, all this came out subtly, through innuendos rather than statements, and we had to really prod and probe to understand the underlying reasons for his behaviour. We spent the next hour massaging his hurt ego, so he left the room happy and we averted the disaster of a good worker leaving us. We have decided to have a Family Day in office from now on, to showcase to employees' families what a wonderful place our organization is.

The phone rings. It's Sid on the line. 'Where are you, Mom? Come quickly, we have to finish that EVED project. Did you pick up the two speakers from Anil's house?'

Oh, fish! I had promised to collect the speakers from his classmate's place and I forgot! And now I can't turn back, since I am stuck in this horrible jam and the only way out is to inch forward.

I make a call to my mother in turn. 'Mom, where are you? Sid needs two speakers for his project and I don't have them!' A frantic wail emanates from me.

My mother's calm voice reassures and soothes and my panic subsides. As a science teacher and an old hand at project-making, I know she will magically convert some old matchboxes and wires and plugs into the required speakers, and all will be fine.

The next call comes from HD, who has, surprisingly, reached

home early. I launch into a litany of my woes, including the present state of suspended animation I am in, on a smog-filled and noisy road in Mumbai. As a fully trained husband ought to, he immediately and gracefully morphs into his sympathetic mode, listening without interjecting and transmitting waves of empathy over the phone. 'Don't worry, sweetie, stay cool and clear your email backlog while you are stuck. I'll organize the food, and a nice drink will be waiting for you when you reach home. See you!'

Later that night, I reflect on the madcap journey of so many years of working, including the various crises of the day, and I wonder if it has been worth it. The stress of working continuously for over two decades, of living in a city coming apart at its seams, the commutes, the difficult bosses, the self-centred subordinates and demanding investors. Have they been worth the trade-off I have made—giving up on a peaceful and uncomplicated life at home, fully dedicated to bringing up son and husband?

And then I see in my mind the pride on my mother's face when she introduces me to her new neighbours, and the sense of complete confidence with which Sid says 'I am also going to run a company, just like you and Papa', and I get that letter from an ex-employee who says he has never found the same enabling environment he got while working with us and wants to come back.

And so, while balancing out the debit and credit parts of these past twenty-odd years, I conclude that in the final analysis the bottom line has only been positive.

I sigh to myself, turn on my side and go to sleep.

Yeeks! I wake up with a start as the alarm goes off shrilly next to me. It's 5.30 a.m. once again...

ACKNOWLEDGEMENTS

My sincere thanks to the following people; this book is theirs as well.

Rachna Kanwar, friend, 'first follower' and colleague, for her faith and for building the connections which made this book a reality.

Kartik Kalla, for his passion and patience in creating the outstanding cover, along with Abhishek Dey of Elevenbrandworks.

Varsha Ojha, for holding the reins of this book's marketing so competently in her hands.

Anvita Nath, Swati Rishi, Rachita Vaid, Aesha Malnika, Aditya Gonsalves, Hrishikesh Gangoli, Kanupriya Agarwal, Archaana Pania, Snigdha Nandan and Keerat Grewal, for putting their collective creative might behind the book and for unravelling the mysteries of the digital world for me.

Pradipta Sarkar, editor par excellence, and everyone at Rupa Publications, for believing in this book and taking control of it so completely.

Satyanarayana Murthy and Binoy Joseph, for helping me create my blog, www.womenatwork.co.in, which became the genesis of this book.

Uday and Kanchan Purohit, Nitin Karkare and Sulekha Bajpai, Divya Oberoi, Satish Chander, Ashit Kukian, Anil Dimri, Ambar Basu, Shailesh Kapoor and, especially, Ashish Gharde, for their constant support and constructive criticism and for just for being there.

All the wonderful women I know, who have been a source of joy (and also of some of the anecdotes here): Arpita Menon, Dnyanada Chaudhari, Nidhi Lall, Sanghamitra Ghosh, Sagorika Kantharia, Reshma Khalid, Deepa Dave, Kalpana Rao, Vishakha Singh, Savita Mathai, Neeta Hemdev, Praveen Malhotra and Anurradha Prasad.

Everyone at Radio City 91.1 FM and IVFA, for being such wonderful colleagues and partners.

Our programming divas, Anurita Patel, Ginnie Mahajan, Maya Iyer and Meenal Sanjagiri, along with Raajiv Patel, for their unstinting support in ensuring that this book reaches out to as many people as possible.

Peter Fernandez, for making life in office that much easier.

My mother-in-law, for bringing up her sons so well.

Scamper, for teaching all of us what unconditional love is and for his great attitude despite his disabilities.

And, finally, Mummy, Sanjay and Siddharth, without whom nothing in life would have been possible.